# CAMBRIDGE MUSICAL TEXTS AND MONOGRAPHS

*General Editors: Howard Mayer Brown,*
*Peter le Huray, John Stevens*

# TREATISE ON HARPSICHORD TUNING
*by*
## JEAN DENIS

# CAMBRIDGE MUSICAL TEXTS AND MONOGRAPHS

*General Editors: Howard Mayer Brown,*
*Peter le Huray, John Stevens*

PUBLISHED
Ian Woodfield *The Early History of the Viol*
*Principles of the Harpsichord by Monsieur de Saint Lambert*
Translated and edited by Rebecca Harris-Warrick
Robin Stowell *Violin Technique and Performance Practice*
*in the Late Eighteenth and Early Nineteenth Centuries*

# TREATISE ON HARPSICHORD TUNING BY JEAN DENIS

*Translated and edited by*
VINCENT J. PANETTA, Jr.

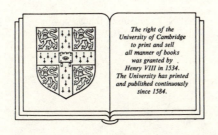

The right of the
University of Cambridge
to print and sell
all manner of books
was granted by
Henry VIII in 1534.
The University has printed
and published continuously
since 1584.

CAMBRIDGE UNIVERSITY PRESS

*Cambridge*
London   New York   New Rochelle
Melbourne   Sydney

Published by the Press Syndicate of the University of Cambridge
The Pitt Building, Trumpington Street, Cambridge CB2 1RP
32 East 57th Street, New York, NY 10022, USA
10 Stamford Road, Oakleigh, Melbourne 3166, Australia

First published 1987

Printed in Great Britain at
the University Press, Cambridge

*British Library cataloguing in publication data*
Denis, Jean
Treatise on harpsichord tuning. –
(Cambridge musical texts and monographs)
1. Harpsichord – Tuning
I. Title II. Panetta, Vincent J.
III. Traité de l'accord de l'espinette.
*English*
786.2'3   MT252

*Library of Congress cataloguing in publication data*
Denis, Jean
Treatise on harpsichord tuning.
(Cambridge musical texts and monographs)
Translation of: Traité de l'accord de l'espinette.
Bibliography.
Includes index.
1. Harpsichord – Tuning. I. Panetta, Vincent J.
II. Title. III. Series.
MT165.D45   1987   786.2'3   86–18396

ISBN 0 521 30628 0 hard covers
ISBN 0 521 31402 X paperback

WD

Art has no authority other than that granted to it by the intellect of man.

Marin Mersenne
*Harmonie universelle*, vol. III, p. 357

# Contents

# Acknowledgments

Margaret Irwin-Brandon of Mount Holyoke College first brought the treatise of Jean Denis to my attention. Howard Mayer Brown was an enthusiastic supporter of this project from the beginning, and offered advice and encouragement at all stages.

Several colleagues were kind enough to read early drafts and offer their criticisms. These readers included Paul Evans and Richard Sherr (Smith College), Edward Parmentier (University of Michigan), Bruce Gustafson (Franklin and Marshall College), Nathan Randall (Princeton University), Frances Fitch (New England Conservatory), and Rebecca Harris-Warrick. Special mention should be made of the contribution of Charles Ferguson, Associate Professor of Modern Languages at Colby College and translator of Dom Bédos. He generously agreed to undertake a close reading of the translation and made many valuable suggestions. For helpful comments and advice I am also indebted to Lewis Lockwood, Harald Vogel, Barbara Owen, Elizabeth Powers, and William Dowd. Evan Bonds provided welcome assistance with the correction of proofs.

I owe a final debt of gratitude to Penny Souster and Victoria Cooper, my editors at Cambridge University Press, who cheerfully and efficiently saw to the endless details of preparing the manuscript for publication.

# Translator's Introduction

# 1

# Jean Denis and the
# *Traité de l'accord de l'espinette*

The *Traité de l'accord de l'espinette*, first published in 1643 and issued in its second and final version in 1650, is the first French treatise devoted exclusively to keyboard performance practice. Jean Denis, the author of the *Traité*, was both a harpsichord maker of renown and the organist of a prominent Paris church. Thus, though he is not a 'learned' theorist in the traditional sense, Denis does qualify as an authority worthy of careful study.

Denis's *Traité* appeared during a time of transition in French theoretical writings, and was one of the harbingers of a new era. The more important French treatises of the sixteenth and early seventeenth centuries were the work of humanists, learned academicians who attempted to relate music to mathematics, philosophy, and the body of knowledge as a whole. They told much of theory, but far less of contemporary practice. Around the middle of the seventeenth century, however, detailed treatises written by musicians and composers began to appear, and these documents placed far more emphasis on practical matters than on the philosophy or aesthetics of music. Among their authors were Bénigne de Bacilly, Guillaume-Gabriel Nivers, Jean Millet, and Jean Denis.

With its comments on such fundamental matters as tuning, ornamentation, and the relationship of organ and choir in liturgy, Denis's treatise was clearly directed to practicing musicians rather than readers interested in the more speculative aspects of music theory. The author deliberately presents himself not as a learned savant, but rather as a skilled and proud practitioner. Indeed, he takes special pains to inform his readers that 'those who consider themselves the most learned are those who commit the greatest errors' in practical matters (p. 89). Unlike many other theorists of his time, Denis eschews references to the 'ancients' and to fifteenth- and sixteenth-century theoretical writings. He does not, he tells us, 'wish to speak of theory at all, but instead of practice and custom'

(p. 66). Rather than quoting the Greeks, he refers to his own experience.

In the first chapter, Denis takes up the question of the tuning of keyboard instruments. He is an ardent advocate of meantone temperament and defends it vigorously against the encroachments of equal temperament, which was then being promoted in Paris and which he describes as 'quite wretched and very harsh to the ear' (p. 68). His tuning instructions are not as precise as those of Marin Mersenne or Michael Praetorius (who were among the first to refer to the use of beats in the setting of temperaments). Nevertheless, the information and instructions Denis presents, interpreted in light of other contemporary sources, leave little doubt that he is referring to standard one-quarter comma meantone temperament.

Denis also makes a valuable contribution to the body of seventeenth-century theoretical writings concerning the use of the organ in Catholic rite. After setting forth the eight *tons* of the church in their orthodox locations, Denis discusses the transpositions commonly employed during his time in order to place the reciting tones of the choir within a compact and convenient range. Owing to the then well-established practice of alternation between organ and choir in various parts of the Mass, the organist had to be well versed in these customary transpositions and well prepared for the often-difficult task of reconciling the choir's chant and the pitch level of the organ music. Denis warns of several unacceptable transpositions, convenient perhaps for the choir but unworkable for the organist due to the absence of certain accidentals in the twelve-note meantone octave. (Most if not all of the meantone-tuned French organs of the period apparently lacked auxiliary keys and pipes for the enharmonic notes D♯ and A♭, an arrangement more commonly found in Germany and Italy.)

The *Traité* includes a section on fugue, a term which in this context more properly connotes 'fugal writing' (and improvisation). Denis refers not to complicated polyphonic structures comparable to those of the later Baroque, but rather to various methods for handling motives in fugal expositions. Such imitative techniques are well represented in the French *livres d'orgue* of the seventeenth and early eighteenth centuries. The two final chapters of the treatise, 'The Proper Manner of Playing the Harpsichord and the Organ' and 'On Bad Habits that Occur Among Those who Play Instruments',

4

Table 1 *Instrument Builders of the Denis Family*

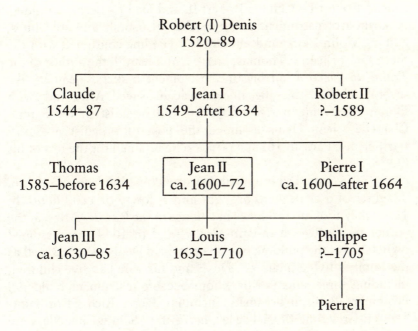

are among the most interesting and enlightening. They offer numerous observations concerning ornamentation, hand position, posture, and related matters. Also included in the work are a short chapter on the various sorts of sounds, a keyboard prelude designed to reveal errors in tuning, and two lively anecdotes attesting to the power of music, both related in delightful style.

The known facts of Jean Denis's life and career can be quickly summarized.[1] Jean Denis (II) was born around the year 1600, into a Parisian family whose members had been builders of stringed keyboard instruments since the middle years of the sixteenth century (see Table 1). His grandfather, Robert I (1520–89), had been a

1 Much of the information presented here concerning members of the Denis family (including Table 1 above) has been drawn from archival references collected by Colombe Samoyault-Verlet in *Les facteurs de clavecins parisiens* (Paris: Société Française de Musicologie, Heugel, 1966), pp. 29–37.

builder of organs as well as *espinettes*, a combination of vocations that was not at all uncommon in sixteenth-century Paris.[2] All three sons of Robert I – Claude, Robert II, and Jean I – became builders of keyboard instruments, though they also built and sold lutes, guitars, violins, kits, and mandoras.[3] The line continued with the three sons of Jean I: Thomas, Pierre I, and Jean II, the author of the *Traité de l'accord*, all became instrument makers.[4] Jean II, like several of his relatives, became a musician as well. After study with Florent Bienvenu, native of Rouen and organist of the Sainte-Chapelle,[5] Jean Denis assumed the post of organist at Saint-Barthélemy, Paris in 1628, a position he retained for the rest of his life.[6]

In 1630, Jean Denis married Antoinette Blondeau of Melun, daughter of a clerk, who brought him a dowry of 1200 *livres*. In 1634, they took up residence in a house in the Rue des Arcis, at the corner of the Rue Jean-Pain-Mollet, and in 1644 they assumed ownership of the building (which contained Denis's shop as well as the family's living quarters). Denis and his wife had five children, including three sons (all of whom became instrument builders). Prominent Parisian organists, including Pierre Richard of Saint-Jean-en-Grève and Michel de la Guerre of the Sainte-Chapelle, were chosen to be godparents at the baptisms of the Denis children.

Little is known of the instrument-building career of Jean Denis beyond several archival references. In 1636, Denis was accused of having struck an apprentice, and by way of compensation he was

---

2 See François Lesure, 'La facture instrumentale à Paris au seizième siècle', *Galpin Society Journal* vii (1954), p. 15; the article was reprinted in *Musique et musiciens français du XVIᵉ siècle* (Geneva: Minkoff Reprint, 1976).

3 The inventories of the shops of Robert II and Claude Denis are reprinted in Lesure, 'La facture instrumentale', pp. 36–42.

4 By the time these three came of age, the sons of makers enjoyed the advantage of not having to serve formal apprenticeships in order to become members of the Parisian instrument makers' guild (whose articles are discussed on pp. 8–9).

5 For more on Florent Bienvenu, see footnote 52 to the translation.

6 The dual career of builder/organist was apparently not unique to the Denis family, nor to the time and place. A number of similar examples from later sixteenth-century Paris have been cited by François Lesure, including that of a Monsieur A. Level, who is listed in 1578 as 'organist at Saint-Barthélemy and builder of *épinettes*'. See Lesure, 'La facture instrumentale', p. 15.

It has often been incorrectly stated that Jean Denis held the post of organist at St.-Séverin, Paris during the last years of his life. The actual holder of the position was his son Jean III. See Samoyault-Verlet, *Les facteurs*, p. 34.

compelled to pay eighteen *livres* to the boy's father.[7] That Denis and Chambonnières were well acquainted is clear from a 1644 reference to a loan of 400 *livres* made by Chambonnières to Denis.[8] The debt, which was repaid in the following year, may well have been related to Denis's purchase of the house in the Rue des Arcis: the loan was made six days before Denis took title to the house. In 1653, Denis was summoned to Nancy to refurbish a harpsichord belonging to the Duchess of Lorraine, an indication perhaps of the esteem accorded his skills by the wealthier classes.[9] Judging from the inventory drawn up after his death in January 1672, the shop of Jean Denis remained active and prosperous even during his later years. In various stages of completion in the shop and household at that time were eight harpsichords, twelve spinets, and two clavichords, as well as several bowed stringed instruments. Also on hand were stocks of cedar and cypress wood, along with a supply of 'fir wood for making soundboards'.[10] Only one of Denis's instruments is known to have survived, that being a rectangular spinet dated 1667 and now housed in the Musée de Varzy, Nièvre. It is a single-manual instrument with a decorated soundboard and jackrail and an apparent range of GG/BB–c′′′.

The Parisian Guild of Master Makers of Musical Instruments (*La Communauté des maîtres faiseurs d'instruments de musique de la ville et faubourgs de Paris*), to which Jean Denis II and his relatives and descendants belonged, was formally chartered on 30 November 1599. The most important provisions of the guild articles can be summarized as follows:[11]

---

7 Archives nationales, Minutier central, II, 152; 7 mai, 1636. Cited in *Documents du Minutier central concernant l'histoire de la musique (1600–1650)*, ed. Madeleine Jurgens (Paris: La Documentation Française, 1969, 1974), vol. I, p. 717.
8 Archives nationales, Minutier central, XII, 79; 16 juin, 1644. Cited in Jurgens (ed.), *Documents du Minutier central*, vol. II, p. 745.
9 Archives départmentales, Meurthe-et-Moselle, B. 1509.
10 Archives nationales, Minutier central, LIV, 356; 12 janvier, 1672. This inventory was reprinted by Norbert Dufourcq in 'Une dynastie française: les Denis', *Revue de Musicologie* xxxviii (1956), pp. 153–5. The inventory was translated by Frank Hubbard in *Three Centuries of Harpsichord Making* (Cambridge, Mass.: Harvard University Press, 1965), Appendix C, pp. 286–7.
11 The 1599 guild statutes, certain of which have been abstracted here, were reprinted in full by Paul Loubet de Sceaury in *Musiciens et facteurs d'instruments de musique sous l'ancien régime* (Paris: Éditions A. Pedone, 1949), pp. 168–71.

– No one was permitted to build or sell instruments in the city of Paris who had not been accepted as a member of the guild. Instruments built or offered for sale in Paris by anyone not a member of the guild, no matter what his profession or rank, could and would be confiscated.

– Conditions for admission to guild membership included satisfactory completion of a six-year apprenticeship in Paris under a master of the guild, and the construction of a *chef d'oeuvre*.[12] Having satisfied these requirements and having demonstrated sound moral character, an applicant could seek the approval of the two *jurés*, or titular wardens, of the guild. Having obtained such approval, he might then be sworn in as a member, after payment of the required fees.

– The sons of guild members were excused from the apprenticeship requirement and from the requirement to build a *chef d'oeuvre*, and could be admitted at the discretion of the *jurés* if found 'capable'.

– Members were allowed to have only one apprentice until that apprentice had served four or more years of his six-year term. A second apprentice could then be hired.

– *Jurés* were nominated and elected by majority vote of the guild members, and served two-year terms.[13]

– No member could maintain more than one *boutique*, no matter what explanations or reasons he might offer, nor could instruments be sold in the streets.

– Surviving widows of deceased members could continue to operate a workshop and retain an apprentice to perform the work, but this right would cease upon the widow's remarriage.

– No member was allowed to make wholesale purchases of materials from abroad without notifying the guild and offering to share these materials with all the other members. Merchandise imported in violation of this rule could be confiscated.

– Members of the guild were free to make cases for their instruments and to ornament them with inlay and marquetry, as they had always done, without interference from anyone.

This last provision, as might have been expected, did not inspire great jubilation among members of the guilds occupied with the making and decorating of furniture. From as early as 1520 comes mention of an incident in which jealous furniture makers entered the shop of an organbuilder and angrily confiscated work in pro-

---

12 Surviving documents record that apprentices began their terms at ages that typically ranged from 12 to 20. In some cases, makers demanded and received fees for taking on new apprentices, and the fees mentioned in the archives range from a low of 18 *livres* to the then-considerable sum of 90 *livres* plus a quantity of wine. See Jurgens (ed.), *Documents du Minutier central*, vol. II, pp. 74–7.

13 Jean Denis was elected to a term as *juré* in 1647.

gress.[14] The formal adoption of guild articles by the instrument makers hardly put an end to such quarrels, and similar disputes were recorded well into the eighteenth century.

Frank Hubbard, in *Three Centuries of Harpsichord Making*, analyzed in memorable fashion the implications of the guild statutes summarized above.

We like to think of the guilds as organizations of ruggedly independent bourgeois, jealous of their privileges and immunities, the cradle of freedom and the school of the arts; but a glance at the guild statute of 1599 will reveal in pitiless detail the basis of economic monopoly and technical restraint on which those organizations rested. To the nepotism implicit in the prohibition of the trade to all who were not members of the guild and the easing of membership qualifications for the sons of masters must be added the methodical elimination of true competition between the masters, and the protection of the incompetent makers at the expense of the talented . . . No maker, even through his own enterprise, could have the advantage of superior materials . . . The limitation of each master to one shop tended to prevent the most talented makers from exploiting their superiority and to reduce all firms to one level . . . The exceedingly slow development until 1775 of all technology including harpsichord making is certainly due in part to the leaden hand of the guilds on the individual artisan. Decades produced only slight improvements, and most makers undoubtedly ended their lives making instruments identical to those which they had studied as apprentices.[15]

The *Traité de l'accord de l'espinette* was first published in a shorter version in 1643, whose text concluded with the words 'End of the first book' (p. 77). The second and final edition, published by Robert Ballard in 1650, incorporated the first edition *in toto* (with minor corrections), and added additional material sufficient to more than double the size of the publication. New to the second edition were the quatrain signed 'R.' (p. 56), the letter of dedication (pp. 57–8), the tuning diagram (p. 72), the *Prelude* (pp. 73–4), and all text after the indication 'End of the first book'.[16]

The uncommon directness of Denis's rather rough-hewn prose sets his treatise apart from similar documents of its time. Despite his occasional expository failings, Denis possesses a knack for fashioning the mordant phrase and delivering the provocatively articulated opinion. We may surmise that he was equally blunt with the spoken

14 Loubet de Sceaury, *Musiciens et facteurs d'instruments*, p. 173.
15 Hubbard, *Three Centuries of Harpsichord Making*, pp. 85–6.
16 See the Introduction by Alan Curtis to the facsimile edition of the *Traité de l'accord de l'espinette* (New York: Da Capo Press, 1969), pp. v–vi, n. 2.

word, for he himself reports that visitors to his shop 'took ill' his frank opinions regarding their playing mannerisms (p. 101).

On the surface at least, Denis projects brash confidence. Much of what he has to say is briskly delivered, in a voice that seems firmly grounded in practical experience and buttressed by no little self-assurance. On the subject of tuning, he avers that 'persons who discuss these matters . . . do not know what they are talking about' (p. 70), and he reserves an especially subtle shade of scorn for the mathematician who has, through clever manipulation of 'numbers', devised a tuning system that results in 'discord' (pp. 63, 69). In his disdain for the 'learned', who make the 'greatest errors', the author's tone verges on arrogance. His occasional attempts to cultivate modesty seem patently affected and entirely disingenuous.

In setting his words to paper, however, Denis ensured that they would be subjected to careful scrutiny, and this clearly troubled him more than a little. He worries that 'people have not been inclined to listen to me, because I am taken for a simple artisan' (p. 70). He spends an entire paragraph ruminating about whether he is qualified to offer advice on harpsichord playing (p. 97), and he frets about the 'experts, who will have the pleasure of deciding whether I have done well' (p. 96). Apparently Denis, a tradesman without the benefit of an advanced education (a fact to which his grammar amply attests), was at least somewhat concerned about his ability to express complicated ideas adequately. We should not be surprised to learn, therefore, that when he came to more difficult issues of music theory, Denis borrowed freely from the published writings of Marin Mersenne.

No correspondence between Denis and Mersenne has survived, and no extant evidence conclusively proves that they were personally acquainted. It is quite clear, however, that they were familiar with each other's works and ideas. Several passages in Mersenne's *Cogitata physico-mathematica* (Paris, 1644) refer to Jean Denis [*Ioannes Dionysius*] and to his talents as a harpsichord builder and tuner.[17] In addition, Mersenne seems to have studied with some care

17 Marin Mersenne, *Cogitata physico-mathematica* (Paris, 1644), pp. 335–6. It is not clear from the context whether the 'Jean Denis' mentioned as one of the 'best makers at present' in Mersenne's *Harmonie universelle* was the author of the *Traité de l'accord* or his father, Jean Denis I (1549–after 1634). The two other builders thus praised in the same sentence were both older men: Jean Jacquet (ca. 1575–1648) and Jacques Le Breton (1589–ca. 1660). See Mersenne, *Harmonie universelle* (Paris, 1636), vol. III, p. 159.

the 1643 first edition of the *Traité de l'accord*; the only surviving copy of the edition (formerly belonging to the library of Mersenne's order, the *Pères Minimes*, and now in the Bibliothèque Mazarine, Paris) bears three marginal annotations which, though largely indecipherable, are almost surely in the hand of Mersenne.[18]

That Denis was intimately familiar with at least some of Mersenne's writings on tuning and temperament becomes evident when Denis's *Traité* is compared to Mersenne's *Nouvelles observations physiques et mathematiques* (Paris, ca. 1638). Of Mersenne's twenty-eight-page essay, five and one-half highly concentrated pages are devoted to a discussion of equal temperament, quarter-comma meantone, and the tuning of keyboard instruments; the pages are among the most cogent of the many that Mersenne devoted to these subjects. Denis borrowed from several passages, sometimes paraphrasing and sometimes copying almost word for word.[19] Though Denis never acknowledges his source, it is clear that he had Mersenne's essay before him as he wrote, and he relied on it to help him negotiate some of the more difficult theoretical territory. Denis's disdain for the 'learned' apparently extended only so far. Nevertheless, these borrowed passages represent only a small part of the entire *Traité*. Denis very definitely possessed a mind of his own, and much of what he has to say appears to be entirely original. It must also be remembered that although Denis borrowed from the printed words of Mersenne, Denis himself, as an authoritative Parisian practitioner, may have originally expounded the ideas in question to Mersenne on one or more occasions (see pp. 29–30 and n. 12 to the translation).

Precisely what audience Denis may have had in mind for the *Traité* is not fully clear. The hope expressed in the author's dedicatory epistle, that his treatise will 'win ... entry into the best households', suggests that he intended his essay, in part at least, for amateur harpsichordists. Indeed, by the 1640s the harpsichord was well on its way to replacing the lute as the favored instrument at court and among the well-to-do. Yet Denis surely envisioned more

18 The pages containing these marginal annotations are reproduced in the Appendix to the facsimile edition of Denis's *Traité* (New York, 1969), pp. 45–9.
19 To permit comparison, the more important of the passages in question are transcribed in Appendix A. See also footnotes 12, 19, 23 and 29 to the translation.

than dilettantes as potential readers. His comment that 'many accomplished harpsichordists and organists . . . would not venture to attempt the tuning of a harpsichord' (p. 64) implies that amateur instrumentalists were not the only ones in need of tuning advice.[20] Even the shorter first edition of the *Traité* included the chapter entitled 'Advice to Choirmasters and Organists', and the 1650 edition added still more pages of text and examples concerning subjects that could only have been of interest to professional church organists: the *tons* of the church and their various transpositions, and the treatment of fugues. He has addressed these subjects, says Denis, in order to offer 'knowledge to those who wish to learn and satisfaction to the experts . . . Those who aspire to mastery will profit therefrom, and will be grateful to me' (p. 96).

The pride and hint of conceit manifest in these last comments suggest that Denis may have conceived the *Traité*, in part at least, as a 'vanity' publication of sorts. For Denis, the obviously proud possessor of so many well-formed opinions, the chance to see his name on a title page and his ideas invested with the authority of print may well have provided sufficient motive for publication. The idea of profiting through the sale of such a treatise was quite possibly secondary to the idea of promoting Jean Denis, and of course his fine instruments as well. As the title page informs us, the work was available for sale at the author's shop, and thus it may represent the original prototype for the tuning and maintenance manuals that modern-day harpsichord builders offer (for a modest fee, of course) along with their instruments.

The Marquis de Mortemart (1600–75), to whom Denis's treatise is dedicated, was a member of an ancient noble family that had taken its name from the village of Mortemart (Haute-Vienne). Gabriel Mortemart was made *Premier Gentilhomme de la Chambre* in 1630, was given the additional titles of Duke and Peer by Louis XIV in 1650, and became Governor of Paris in 1669. According to the *Grand dictionnaire universel* of Pierre Larousse (Paris, 1874), he was 'one of the kindest, best educated, and most

---

20 Indeed, Mersenne even suggests that 'many' builders of harpsichords and organs were themselves unable to tune the instruments they constructed. See Mersenne, *Nouvelles observations*, p. 23. It is impossible to know whether Mersenne was speaking from direct experience or merely repeating a sardonic pronouncement made by the likes of Jean Denis.

intelligent men at court'. Judging from the evidence of Denis's dedication, Mortemart was also an amateur musician of some skill. He left one son, the Duc de Vivonne, and four daughters, three of whom became quite renowned: the Abbesse de Fontevrault, the Marquise de Thianges, and Madame de Montespan. Beyond the evidence of the dedication to the *Traité*, nothing whatever is known regarding the connection between Denis and Mortemart. We should not be surprised, however, that a tradesman like Denis had both the opportunity to meet and the motive to cultivate persons of noble birth. Such individuals were likely to have been among his most valued customers, and in many cases they probably entrusted regular requillings, maintenance, and even tunings of their instruments to him, affording him entry into their households.

# 2

# Jean Denis and meantone temperament

Denis's *Traité* is of special interest because it offers one of the first detailed descriptions of functional keyboard temperament to have been written by a practitioner rather than a theorist. Among French sources, Guillaume Costeley had described a system identical to one-third comma[1] meantone in 1570, but only in reference to an experimental nineteen-note octave.[2] He provided no account of the actual tuning procedure and his ideas, as will be seen, were somewhat outside the mainstream of eventual developments in France and in Europe as a whole. Titelouze had made a brief reference to the necessity for keyboard temperament in the Preface to the *Hymnes de l'Eglise* (Paris, 1623),[3] but he provided no details, instead referring his readers to the writings of earlier theorists ('*les bons auteurs*'). Mersenne had discussed keyboard temperament in exhaustive detail in the *Harmonie universelle*, but there is little evidence in his writings to suggest that he had ever tuned a harpsichord himself. Indeed, his lack of direct familiarity with tuning procedure may well have led to the confusion that crept into his instructions for setting quarter-comma meantone temperament.[4]

Through Denis's frequent references to his temperament system as 'our' tuning and 'our familiar harmonic tuning', we may infer that he clearly has in mind the system of common practice during his day. Unfortunately for modern readers eager for enlightenment and

1 Such references to fractional parts of the syntonic comma (21.506 cents) reflect the amount by which tempered fifths are narrowed in the various sorts of meantone temperament.

2 Guillaume Costeley, *Musique* (Paris, 1570). The Preface that includes the discussion of keyboard temperament has been transcribed and translated by Kenneth Levy in 'Costeley's Chromatic Chanson', *Annales musicologiques, Moyen-Age et Renaissance* iii (1955), pp. 214–15.

3 Jehan Titelouze, *Hymnes de l'Eglise pour toucher sur l'orgue avec les fugues et recherches sur leur plain-chant* (Paris, 1623).

4 See Mark Lindley, 'Temperaments', *The New Grove Dictionary of Music and Musicians* (1980), vol. xviii, p. 664, and 'Mersenne on Keyboard Tuning', *Journal of Music Theory* xxiv (1980), pp. 175–9.

definitive answers, his description of the temperament he recommends with such enthusiasm is not precise. The fifths, he says, are to be narrowed by 'a bit' [un poinct] and the thirds are to be 'good' (p. 66). These seemingly inconclusive criteria appear to leave open a considerable number of possibilities. Nevertheless, by carefully weighing both Denis's statements and relevant information from other sources, we can gradually eliminate from consideration all but one of the tuning systems proposed and discussed by sixteenth- and seventeenth-century writers. In the end, as will be seen, it is possible to conclude with confidence that the temperament advocated by Jean Denis is standard one-quarter comma meantone.

That Denis is referring to some form of meantone temperament can be readily established. First of all, the temperament presented in the *Traité* is a *regular* temperament. By definition, regular temperaments are those in which the size of the fifth does not vary, and Denis unequivocally specifies that all fifths 'are to be tempered equally, all in like manner' (p. 66). It is thus confirmed at the outset that Denis is not recommending one of the many just tuning systems propounded in the sixteenth and seventeenth centuries (all of which are irregular),[5] nor any form of irregular temperament such as the scheme described in 1511 by Arnolt Schlick, which was a closed system of twelve unequally sized fifths.[6] Nor is Denis presenting an irregular system analogous to the temperaments later described in France by Lambert Chaumont, Michel Corrette, Jean-Philippe Rameau, and others.[7] With the establishment of regular temperament as the first criterion, we have reduced the field of possibilities for Denis's temperament to Pythagorean tuning, equal temperament, and the various types of meantone temperament.

Pythagorean tuning is accomplished by tuning a series of pure fifths, and consequently Denis's stipulation that fifths are to be 'narrowed' eliminates Pythagorean tuning from consideration.

---

5 See J. Murray Barbour, *Tuning and Temperament* (East Lansing: Michigan State College Press, 1953), pp. 89–105.

6 Arnolt Schlick, *Spiegel der Orgelmacher und Organisten* (Mainz, 1511; facsimile with translation by Elizabeth Barber. Buren, Netherlands: Frits Knuf, 1980), pp. 73–91 (Knuf edition). See also Heinrich Husmann, 'Zur Charakteristik der Schlickschen Temperatur', *Archiv für Musikwissenschaft* xxiv (1967), pp. 253–65.

7 See Pierre-Yves Asselin, 'Le tempérament en France au 18ᵉ siècle', in *L'Orgue à notre époque*, ed. Donald Mackey (Montreal: McGill University, 1981).

Equal temperament results in a scale of twelve semitones equal in size, but such equally sized semitones are not a feature of Denis's scale. The *Table* of scale intervals in the *Traité* (p. 60) shows two sizes of semitone: a smaller minor semitone ('chromatic' in modern usage), as in the intervals C–C♯ and E♭–E, and a larger major (or 'diatonic') semitone, as in the interval C♯–D. Semitones of different sizes preclude equal temperament.

In addition, Denis's temperament defines a tonal system that includes only the pitches in a series of narrowed fifths beginning at E♭ and extending to G♯, the note that is the 'end of the tuning' (p. 66). The remaining interval G♯–E♭ (a diminished sixth far too wide to be musically useful) is the *'deffaut de l'accord'* (p. 72). Thus there is no question of equal temperament, or *any* temperament with a closed circle of fifths. The characterization of Denis as an advocate of equal temperament, first put forth by Murray Barbour[8] and subsequently taken up by other writers, should be permanently laid to rest. Beyond the evidence just cited, there is also Denis's own eloquent report of his reaction to a demonstration of equal temperament, which he compares most unfavorably with the system he himself advocates (pp. 68–9). Finally, there is the testimony of Mersenne, who observes in the *Cogitata physico-mathematica* that

... those of us with a more delicate sense of hearing, such as the highly talented instrument maker [*lyropoios*] Denis, can barely tolerate the temperament of equal semitones, though it satisfied other very experienced musicians.[9]

Thus the field of possibilities for Denis's temperament has been narrowed to the various systems of regular meantone temperament. The 'mean' in the expression 'meantone' refers to the fact that all the meantone systems divide the major third (whether it is pure, larger than pure, or smaller than pure) into two whole tones of equal size. In standard one-quarter comma meantone, for example, the whole tone results from a division of the pure 5:4 major third into two equal tones by geometric mean proportional ($\sqrt{5}/2$ or $\sqrt{5/4}$). The resulting whole tones are of a mean size (and their ratio a geometric

8 Barbour, *Tuning and Temperament*, p. 47.
9 Mersenne, *Cogitata physico-mathematica*, p. 335.

mean) between the 9:8 (major) and 10:9 (minor) tones of theoretical just intonation.[10]

Quarter-comma meantone was by far the best known and most frequently discussed of the many meantone schemes. As a keyboard temperament, it enjoyed wide use throughout Europe during much of the sixteenth and seventeenth centuries, and persisted in certain English organs until well into the nineteenth century. The system is based on pure major thirds and on fifths narrowed by one-quarter (5.38 cents) of the syntonic comma (81:80, or 21.506 cents, and also known as the comma of Didymus). Eleven fifths are so tuned, with the accumulated error of the cycle left to the last 'fifth', G♯–E♭ (actually a diminished sixth, as noted above). This interval, referred to by Praetorius and others as the 'wolf', is one and three-quarters commas wider than pure, or 737.6 cents in size, compared to the narrow 696.6-cent size of the other eleven fifths in the temperament. The wolf can theoretically be placed anywhere in the meantone octave. In practice it seems most often to have been placed in the remote G♯–E♭ location, though it was sometimes shifted to D♯–B♭ (creating a D♯ to replace the E♭ ordinarily tuned), or to C♯–A♭ (creating an A♭ to replace the usual G♯).[11]

During the sixteenth and seventeenth centuries, a number of meantone schemes besides the quarter-comma system were also proposed by theorists. The most prominent among these were temperaments that narrowed the fifths by (in increasing order of diminishment) one-sixth, one-fifth, two-sevenths, and one-third of the syntonic comma.[12] None of these systems offers pure major thirds, though as noted above, all share in common the division of the major third,

---

10 A practical method for accomplishing this division of the major third is presented by Francisco de Salinas in the *De musica libri septem* (Salamanca, 1577), pp. 158–9.

11 In the *Musicalische Temperatur* (Quedlinburg, 1691), pp. 1–2 and *passim*, Andreas Werckmeister asserts that quarter-comma meantone temperament is '*falsch*' and outmoded, and he presents a laughable distortion of the temperament with the wolf placed at f–c'. The context must be taken into account, however, for in the following pages Werckmeister presses the case for his own newly devised systems for keyboard temperament.

12 Later versions of meantone mentioned by Marpurg, Romieu, and others divided the syntonic comma into seven, eight, nine, and ten parts, resulting in increasingly wide major thirds. The intervals of theoretical one-eleventh comma meantone are nearly identical to those of equal temperament, which divides the Pythagorean comma (23.5 cents) into twelve parts.

Table 2 A Comparison of Temperament Systems

| Temperament System | Fifth | Fifth, Cents | Major Third | Major Third, Cents | Minor Third | Minor Third, Cents | Diatonic Semitone, Cents | Chromatic Semitone, Cents | G#–E♭ 'Wolf' Fifth, Cents |
|---|---|---|---|---|---|---|---|---|---|
| 1/3–Comma Meantone | −1/3[a] | 695 | −1/3 | 379 | Pure | 316 | 126 | 63 | 758 |
| 2/7–Comma Meantone | −2/7 | 696 | −1/7 | 383 | −1/7 | 313 | 121 | 71 | 746 |
| 1/4–Comma Meantone | −1/4 | 696.6 | Pure | 386.3 | −1/4 | 310.3 | 117.1 | 76 | 737.6 |
| 1/5–Comma Meantone | −1/5 | 698 | +1/5 | 391 | −2/5 | 307 | 112 | 84 | 726 |
| 1/6–Comma Meantone | −1/6 | 699 | +1/3 | 394 | −1/2 | 305 | 108 | 89 | 721 |
| Equal Temperament | −1/11 | 700 | +5/8 | 400 | −3/4 | 300 | 100 | 100 | — |
| Just Interval Size | | 702 | | 386.3 | | 316 | 112 | 71 | |

[a]Fractions in the table refer to the portion of the syntonic comma (21.5 cents) added to or subtracted from the interval in question.

whatever its size, into two whole tones of equal size. Table 2 will facilitate comparison of these various systems.

Of the four different kinds of meantone temperament just mentioned, the one-third comma system can be eliminated almost immediately from consideration as the temperament of Denis, since it is entirely unsuitable for an octave of twelve notes. A bit of its interesting story will be related, however, because of its history of connections with French composers and theorists. The one-third comma scheme was well known in the latter half of the sixteenth century, and was mentioned in 1571 by Gioseffo Zarlino[13] (though not discussed in detail) and in 1577 by Francisco de Salinas.[14] Though the system includes pure minor thirds, it also features exceedingly narrow major thirds and fifths. Nevertheless, it does possess the virtue of being easy to tune and to set on a monochord. Furthermore, a cycle of fifths so narrowed very nearly closes at nineteen, resulting in a circulating temperament of nineteen virtually equal microtones (with whole tones divided into three parts and *mi–fa* major semitones into two parts). The nineteen-note equal division and the one-third comma meantone system are for all practical purposes one and the same.[15] References to keyboard instruments possessing nineteen notes per octave began to appear in the mid sixteenth century, and such references are frequent enough to indicate that one-third comma meantone and similar arrangements held a certain fascination for theorists and practitioners, an appeal that paralleled the long-lived interest in the possibilities of realizing intervals of the chromatic and enharmonic genera on keyboard instruments.

It is likely that the one-third comma temperament system was introduced to France through the influence of Guillaume Costeley, who in fact makes reference to the system even earlier than either Zarlino or Salinas. In Costeley's *Musique* (Paris, 1570) there appears a *chanson spirituelle* entitled *Seigneur Dieu ta pitié*. The Preface to the collection includes the following discussion.

---

13 Gioseffo Zarlino, *Dimostrationi harmoniche* (Venice, 1571), pp. 218–22.
14 Salinas, *De musica libri septem*, pp. 143–8.
15 For a detailed numerical comparison of the two temperaments, see Joel Mandelbaum, 'Multiple Division of the Octave and the Tonal Resources of 19-Tone Temperament' (Unpublished dissertation, Indiana University, 1961), p. 108.

... As to the chanson that begins *Seigneur Dieu ta pitié*, I composed it twelve years ago as a sort of experiment with the notion of a music sweeter and more agreeable than the diatonic when nicely worked out. For the most part its tones are divided only by thirds, whereby it can readily be seen that the organ and the harpsichord are indeed far from perfect in their construction, since it is necessary to add, within an octave or diapason containing eight naturals and five accidentals, a further seven accidentals, thus making twelve accidentals in all, distributed among the eight naturals. This a good maker could arrange without enlarging the keyboard, which must always remain in its familiar proportion to the hand. The naturals and accidentals will thus be graduated by equal intervals of a third of a tone, from one end to the other, thus offering the means to realize something admirably agreeable and new ... I am not speaking of semitones at all, for so long as the instrument is arranged in the above manner these will not be found at all.[16]

By Costeley's own testimony, then, the *chanson* was composed in the same year (1558) as *Le istitutioni harmoniche* of Zarlino was published, in which a harpsichord of nineteen notes per octave is illustrated for the first time.[17] Zarlino, however, does not mention the one-third comma meantone system in this edition, but refers instead to the two-sevenths comma system discussed below. Costeley seems to have been the first to advocate the nineteen-note equal/one-third comma meantone system. As to the source of Costeley's inspiration, it has been suggested that the nineteen-note system may have been derived from certain monochord divisions of Aristoxenus and Ptolemy that were mentioned by Boethius and Glareanus, among others.[18]

The nineteen-note equal division is also mentioned in French sources of the seventeenth century, in connection with the organist Jehan Titelouze.[19] In a letter of 2 March 1622 to Mersenne, Titelouze writes, in response to a question about composing in the three genres of music:

... the enharmonic would be very difficult to notate with our characters. Out

---

16 Costeley, *Musique*, Preface. The word *espinette* in original texts has been translated throughout this Introduction as 'harpsichord', unless it is clear that 'spinet' in particular is meant. See 'Notes on the Translation', pp. 51–2.
17 Zarlino, *Le istitutioni harmoniche* (Venice, 1558), p. 141.
18 Levy, 'Costeley's Chromatic Chanson', pp. 221–2.
19 Titelouze may well have learned about the temperament from Costeley himself, for it seems quite likely that the two were acquainted; in 1601, Costeley was summoned to Rouen to judge alterations that had been made by organbuilder Crespin Carlier to the instrument at the city's Cathedral, where Titelouze was organist.

of curiosity, I have used it in a piece that I play on a certain specially made harpsichord, but because of this difficulty I am unable to render it in writing.[20]

This in itself does not provide specific evidence of the instrument or temperament that Titelouze had in mind. In May 1625, however, Mersenne visited Titelouze in Rouen. There he presumably saw this 'specially made' instrument and heard the explanation of its tuning, for he later writes in the *Harmonie universelle*:

One can also divide the tone into three equal parts, as Titelouze has done on a special harpsichord which he played for me.[21]

Mersenne also remarks, in the *Livre troisiesme des Genres*:

I will add that if one prefers to divide each tone into three or four parts to play the enharmonic, that each person is free to do as he pleases . . . and thus each third of a tone will be almost 25:24, that is to say a minor semitone, as is seen in this division of the tone into three parts that approach equality [the 9:8 tone is shown divided into three tones of 27:26, 26:25, 25:24] . . . which I wanted to point out on behalf of an excellent organist who used to employ this division on a harpsichord . . . [22]

What is most important to our discussion here, however, is the clear fact that one-third comma meantone adapts itself poorly to an octave of twelve notes (as Costeley himself points out in the Preface quoted above). Triadic harmonies in particular are unsatisfactory, due to the unusually narrow fifths and major thirds, and there is little evidence that this temperament ever achieved other than theoretical and experimental acceptance. At least one noted commentator ascribed little worth to the scheme, even when applied on a special instrument. Giovanni Battista Doni, in a letter of 7 August 1638 to Mersenne, offered the following opinion of Titelouze's demonstration:

I must confess to you frankly that I wondered whether you had been misled in this experiment M. Titelouze presented to you. For if the sound of that harpsichord was good, it surely did not, believe me, have the tones divided into three equal parts, but rather according to the ordinary tuning, in which the middle interval of the three tones C–C♯, C♯–D♭, D♭–D (namely the lesser diesis) is much smaller than the two others.[23]

20 *Correspondance du P. Marin Mersenne* (ed. Cornelius de Waard et al., Paris: Presses Universitaires de France, 1945–83), vol. I, p. 75.
21 Mersenne, *Harmonie universelle*, vol. II, p. 439.
22 Mersenne, *Harmonie universelle*, vol. II, p. 196.
23 *Correspondance du P. Marin Mersenne*, vol. VII, pp. 17–18.

The next form of meantone we shall consider is the two-sevenths comma system, a temperament first described in 1558 by Gioseffo Zarlino.[24] Like the previous system, this one appears to be associated with an attempt to provide for intervals of the enharmonic genus on a keyboard instrument. In connection with his discussion, Zarlino presents the above-mentioned woodcut illustration of a harpsichord with nineteen notes to the octave, specially constructed for him in 1548 by 'Maestro Domenico Pesarese' (Domenico of Pesaro). Though Zarlino's text is not clear on the point, it was presumably upon this instrument that the two-sevenths comma system was employed.[25] This arrangement, however, is also unsatisfactory for triadic harmony when applied to an octave of twelve notes. In addition, the temperament is difficult to set with precision, since the 25:24 chromatic semitone is the only just interval. The two-sevenths comma scheme seems to have attracted little attention in the seventeenth century, and no mention is made of it in French sources. Toward the end of the century it is briefly discussed and dismissed by Andreas Werckmeister who, with a mind to promoting his own systems for circulating temperament, typically presents alternative systems with their wolf fifths placed in the worst possible locations.

Zarlino thought a good temperament could be derived from tuning all fifths impure by two-sevenths of the comma. But this cannot be done. Even when all fifths are tuned impure by one-seventh of the comma, the last fifth, F–c (if one starts on C) differs by being four-sevenths too large, something rather hard to take with one's ear.[26]

The choices for the identity of Denis's temperament have now been narrowed to three prime candidates: the one-quarter comma, one-fifth comma, and one-sixth comma[27] meantone temperaments.

---

24 Zarlino, *Le istitutioni harmoniche*, pp. 139–42.
25 Harpsichords with nineteen notes per octave could have been satisfactorily tuned in at least three different ways: in either one-third or two-sevenths comma meantone, or by extension of quarter-comma meantone temperament through the tuning of additional pure major thirds, adding the usually absent notes D♭, D♯, G♭, A♭, and A♯, and tuning the two remaining notes between E–F and B–C as E♯ or F♭ and B♯ or C♭ respectively. For more on keyboard instruments with divided accidentals, see pp. 36–43.
26 Andreas Werckmeister, *Erweiterte und verbesserte Orgel-Probe* (Quedlinburg, 1698; trans. Gerhard Krapf. Raleigh: The Sunbury Press, 1976), p. 80 (original), pp. 66–7 (translation). Krapf translation quoted here. See also n. 11.
27 This temperament later became associated with the German organbuilder Gottfried Silbermann (1683–1753). See Helmut Lange, 'Über die Bedeutung des syntonischen

It should be stressed that there is no conclusive evidence in the *Traité de l'accord* that could definitively eliminate any of these three from consideration. As noted above, Denis himself indicates only that the major thirds must be 'good', and that the fifths must be diminished by 'a bit' [*un poinct*], a description that could nicely apply to any of the above three varieties of meantone temperament. As Table 2 shows, both one-fifth and one-sixth comma meantone temperaments possess moderately tempered fifths and major thirds larger than pure. These widened major thirds, however, are considerably smaller than those of equal temperament and well within the range of what might be considered 'good'.

Only quarter-comma meantone possesses pure major thirds, which would perhaps best satisfy the requirement of goodness, but Denis nowhere mentions the pure third as a criterion. He does state that the tuning 'is proven only by the thirds. When they are good throughout, then the tuning is correct' (p. 71). Nowhere, however, does he state that these thirds should be pure, only that they should be 'good'. It could perhaps be said of Denis (as Mark Lindley has remarked of Pietro Aaron) that though he would not have faulted quarter-comma meantone, neither did he specify it.[28] Indeed, by 1698, Étienne Loulié avers that one-fifth comma meantone is 'better and more in use' in France than any other form of temperament, an opinion echoed in 1707 by Joseph Sauveur.[29] Their comments, however, refer to the practices of a later era. From the middle years of the seventeenth century, a considerable body of evidence can be cited which, considered as a whole, strongly suggests that Denis is in fact referring specifically to quarter-comma meantone.

By consulting other French sources of Denis's time, it is possible to form an idea of the predominant keyboard temperament of the period. Marin Mersenne, through the ample testimony of his collected correspondence, was in frequent contact with musical figures of his era and questioned them closely on matters he intended to dis-

Kommas und seine Verwendung in der Orgelstimmung Gottfried Silbermanns', *Acta Organologica* xvi (1982), pp. 235–48.

28 A close reading of Aaron reveals that according to his method, only the C–E major third is specifically designated as pure. See Mark Lindley, 'Early 16th-Century Keyboard Temperaments', *Musica Disciplina* xxviii (1974), p. 141.

29 Lindley, 'Temperaments', *The New Grove*, vol. xviii, p. 666.

cuss in published works.[30] Thus his opinions carry special weight. Though he does, in the context of keyboard instruments, discuss equal temperament, systems for just intonation, and a variety of experimental scale divisions involving up to thirty-two microtones per octave, he also makes it abundantly clear that in terms of actual practice, quarter-comma meantone was the usual keyboard temperament employed in his day. In the *Harmonie universelle*, the sixth chapter of the *Livre sixiesme des orgues* begins as follows:

PROPOSITION XVI.

To explain the easiest and most perfect Diapason of the Organ that could be imagined, although temperament is employed . . . and consequently to set out the manner of tuning ordinary Organs perfectly . . .

Since I have shown that the keyboard and the octave that contain the diatonic genus, as currently used in its perfection, have 32, 27, 25, or at the least 19 keys or degrees in each octave, and since the usual keyboards of organs and harpsichords have but 13,[31] it follows that they cannot be just if one wishes to find everything in them that is found in the 19 degrees of the perfect keyboard.

That is why one is compelled to augment or diminish most of the intervals, both dissonant and consonant. And since the difference between the major and minor tones cannot be retained, they are made equal, such that there is no difference between the tones on the organ.[32] It is for this reason that the major tone is diminished by half of a comma, by which quantity the minor tone is augmented. Thus it follows that the major thirds retain their perfection. Since the interval of the major third is divided proportionally, there are two equal tones, of which one is augmented by as much as the other is diminished.

And because the octave is always perfect, and the minor sixth makes the octave with the major third, it follows that this sixth has its just proportion . . . the minor third . . . is diminished by the fourth part of a comma, since it is composed of a major tone and a major semitone when it is perfect. The major tone is diminished by a half comma and the major semitone is augmented by one-quarter of the same comma, because it is made up of the minor semitone (which in this temperament is augmented by one-quarter comma), and the diesis, which suffers no alteration, and consequently the minor third is too small by one-quarter of a comma.

The fifth is also too small by one-quarter of a comma, because it is composed of the two thirds, and the fourth is too large by the same one-quarter comma, because it makes the octave with the fifth.[33]

30 The authorities with whom Mersenne corresponded included Titelouze, Doni, Constantin Huygens, Joan-Albert Ban, Antoine Parran, and Pierre Trichet. In several of these cases, the relatively few extant letters hint at more extensive correspondence that has not survived.
31 This is a reference to a standard octave; Mersenne has simply counted C twice to arrive at the total of thirteen keys.
32 Mersenne refers to equal whole tones, not equal semitones.
33 Mersenne, *Harmonie universelle*, vol. III, p. 341.

This is a clear and unequivocal description of quarter-comma meantone temperament, and it is important to note that it is presented not as 'a method', but as *the* method for the tuning of ordinary organs (by which Mersenne means organs with the customary twelve notes per octave). In *Proposition XXIX* of the same *Livre sixiesme des orgues*, Mersenne goes on to explain the step-by-step procedure for setting this temperament in organs, and again it is expressly stated that the fifths must be diminished by one-quarter of a comma.

Mersenne's instructions in the *Harmonie universelle* for the tuning of keyboard instruments are not precise, and are in fact marred by error. These circumstances should not, however, divert us from the perception of his basic intent. The error arises in *Proposition I* of the *Livre troisiesme des instruments à chordes*. There the author, in the midst of an abbreviated description of spinet-tuning procedure, suddenly announces that ' . . . the fifths must be divided into major and minor thirds, such that the major thirds are a bit diminished and the minor thirds are a bit wider than their justness demands'.[34] This odd prescription must be dismissed as an obvious mistake. Thirds altered in such a manner are found in no documented system of temperament, and minor thirds enlarged beyond purity would result in major thirds so small as to be intolerable.

With the exception of that error, no other comment is made in the *Harmonie universelle* on the specific sizes of the intervals to be employed in the tuning of stringed keyboard instruments. Instead we find the following:

I come now to the tuning of the spinet, which is the same as the tuning of the organ, for it has as many keys in each octave as the organ does. That is why I shall say here only that one should approach as closely as possible the purity of each consonance, which is the objective of every sort of temperament. But I leave the rest for the treatise on the organ.[35]

From this we may conclude that Mersenne regarded the temperament systems for organs and stringed keyboard instruments to be identical. There is further confirmation that this system was the quarter-comma meantone system. In *Observation VII* of the

34 Mersenne, *Harmonie universelle*, vol. III, p. 105.
35 Mersenne, *Harmonie universelle*, vol. III, p. 104.

*Nouvelles observations physiques et mathematiques*, Mersenne once again affirms that fifths are tempered 'the same on the organ as on the harpsichord', and that the musicians who play organs and harpsichords greatly value 'the perfection of their thirds, and also their [unequal] semitones, which lend great beauty and variety to music'.[36] In sum, it is clear that according to the most reliable authority of Denis's time, organs and harpsichords shared the same temperament system: one-quarter comma meantone temperament.

In both editions of the *Traité de l'accord*, Jean Denis also affirms that organs and harpsichords are tuned in the same fashion.

The tuning of the harpsichord is the same as that of the organ. There is no difference, and the practitioners of each agree on this point. When I speak of one, I speak of the other as well. (p. 64)

It seems entirely unreasonable to suppose that Denis, writing only a few years later than Mersenne and in the very same city, assumes a universal keyboard tuning system that is substantially different from Mersenne's. There is, in fact, virtually no evidence to suggest that this was Denis's intent, for never once does he describe his system with such adjectives as 'new' or 'different', nor does he set it forth as an improvement over some existing scheme. Denis's above-cited references to 'our tuning' and 'our familiar harmonic tuning' hardly seem the designations that would have been employed by an author eager to present to the world a tuning system somehow at variance with contemporary practice, the practice that had been specified so explicitly by Mersenne.

Nevertheless, we must confront the fact that Denis never mentions the pure major third as a feature of his temperament. Moreover, his method for the actual tuning of the instrument does nothing to exploit the ease that the pure third can bring to the setting of a quarter-comma meantone bearing. In the simplest approach to such a procedure, the only intervals that actually need to be tempered are the first four fifths, each by one-quarter of the syntonic comma. The remaining seven notes of the scale, both naturals and accidentals, can then be tuned by means of pure major thirds from the five diatonic notes already tuned. Though it would

36 Mersenne, *Nouvelles observations*, p. 20.

seem far easier to temper four fifths than to temper eleven, Denis's method for setting meantone temperament nevertheless depends entirely on fifths, each of which needs to be narrowed with great accuracy. The procedure as presented by Denis does not rule out quarter-comma meantone, but at the same time it leaves open the additional possibilities of one-fifth or one-sixth comma meantones. Yet in view of the evidence from Mersenne cited above, neither of these other meantone systems seems likely to have been the common-practice temperament referred to by Denis. A closer look at the difficulties of setting quarter-comma meantone temperament suggests a possible explanation for Denis's avoidance of the pure major third in his tuning instructions.

Because of the many pure thirds in each octave, quarter-comma meantone has acquired an unjustified reputation as an easy temperament to set. It is in fact an especially difficult temperament to set accurately, since the fifths must all be diminished by precisely the same amount. Because the fifths of quarter-comma meantone are narrowed (and the fourths widened) as much as the ear can reasonably tolerate, there is scant margin for error. Inaccuracy in the setting of even one fifth will spawn a host of sour intervals, which are particularly noticeable in the treble range of a keyboard instrument. These circumstances help to explain Denis's remark (p. 64) that 'many accomplished harpsichordists and organists . . . would not venture to attempt the tuning of a harpsichord', and they also help to explain the emphasis placed on the meantone fifth by theorists other than Denis.

In Volume II of the *Syntagma Musicum*, published in 1619, Michael Praetorius presents three different procedures for tempering keyboard instruments in quarter-comma meantone, accompanied by detailed discussion. In all three of these cases (and particularly in the second method given), the temperament is set primarily with octaves and fifths, with thirds being employed to check for accuracy. The precise tempering of the fifths, says Praetorius:

. . . is the most difficult but most important operation. An entire instrument can be tuned solely by means of octaves and fifths, with major thirds used as checks . . . [37]

---

37 Michael Praetorius, *Syntagma Musicum* (Wolfenbüttel, 1619), vol. II, p. 151.

In the *Harmonie universelle*, Mersenne also presents keyboard tuning instructions that employ no major thirds, but only octaves and fifths, though it is abundantly clear in these instances that Mersenne, like Praetorius, is referring to the quarter-comma variety of meantone.[38] Thus, the lack of mention of the pure third is not, by itself, proof that Denis is not referring to a quarter-comma scheme. In *Proposition XXIX* of the *Livre sixiesme des orgues*, Mersenne provides further clarification. After stating that a good ear is the first requisite for proper tuning, he continues as follows:

In the second place, it must be remarked that the ear perceives the imperfection of consonances more easily than that of dissonances, since perfection is farther from imperfection than imperfection is from itself (though this proposition is not without many complications that deserve further discussion). Thus it happens that one more often tunes with consonances than with dissonances. It is for this same reason that the most agreeable and easiest to understand are chosen, as I will show below.[39]

After the octave (in which every partial of the upper note is, in theory at least, a unison with a partial of the lower note), the 'most agreeable and easiest to understand' consonance is the fifth. Of all consonances, the major third is one of the most difficult in which to judge temperament, a phenomenon first discussed formally by Sauveur in 1707[40] and also alluded to in 1619 by Praetorius, who recommends tuning tenths rather than thirds.[41] Within the first two octaves of overtones in a major third, the upper partials of each constituent note are four times located a minor second apart; thus there is a suggestion of dissonance even when the interval is perfectly just. This effect was perhaps also noted by Mersenne and may have accounted for the reasoning cited above, though at the conclusion of *Proposition XXIX* he points out that 'makers and organists', presumably experienced, do indeed customarily tune with both major and minor thirds as well as fourths.

This can be explained and understood much more quickly and easily if each octave is divided into its four intervals . . . for example, one tunes all at once

38 Mersenne, *Harmonie universelle*, vol. III, pp. 108–9, 364–6.
39 Mersenne, *Harmonie universelle*, vol. III, p. 363.
40 Joseph Sauveur, 'Methode générale pour former les systêmes temperés de musique, & du choix de celui qu'on doit suivre', *Histoire de l'Académie royale des sciences* [1707] (Paris 1730), *Memoires*, p. 219; facsimile reprint in *Joseph Sauveur: Collected Writings on Musical Acoustics*, ed. Rudolf Rasch (Utrecht: The Diapason Press, 1984).
41 Praetorius, *Syntagma Musicum*, vol. II, p. 155.

and with the same hand C, E, G, and C . . . But one must have a better ear to tune by thirds than by fifths. I am omitting the other methods of tuning that might be imagined, with tones and semitones, in order to explain how one may perceive whether the fifths in the tuning are properly tempered, that is to say, whether they are sufficiently narrowed. Though I have shown elsewhere that they must be diminished by a quarter of a comma, it is nevertheless difficult to perceive this diminution since it requires a good ear, which many lack.[42]

In other words, Marin Mersenne, like Praetorius, considers the fifth to be the critical interval in setting quarter-comma meantone, and has based his instructions around it. Given Denis's tendency to follow the reasonings and even the very phrasings of Mersenne's published writings,[43] it does not seem unreasonable to conjecture that Denis might also have modeled the tuning instructions in the *Traité* on those Mersenne had published, complete with the emphasis on the fifth rather than the third – though Denis himself quite possibly employed the major third when he himself tuned, as Mersenne suggests in the above reference to 'makers and organists'.

Additional important evidence that Denis had quarter-comma meantone in mind remains to be cited. In the 1644 *Cogitata physico-mathematica*, Mersenne once more provides instructions for the tuning of stringed keyboard instruments in quarter-comma meantone. These instructions are direct and practical, and are far more lucid and concise than any others Mersenne had previously supplied. Jean Denis figures importantly in this chapter, as the following passage attests.

. . . it should first be known that the ear of the practitioner (such as the above-mentioned Jean Denis, who builds harpsichords and brings them into tune more perfectly than anyone) is so educated that it can perceive 1/136 part of the sound when tempering the fifth in organs or harpsichords, which is close to one-quarter of the comma[44] . . . the only way the fifth is perceived to be this part of a comma away from perfect is through the warring or beating of sounding strings or pipes. First the strings (or pipes) are brought to the just fifth, and then the little tuning pins or pegs . . . are turned and lowered sufficiently that [the strings] beat just so much, to the extent that sweeter and more perfect harmony is brought to strings and pipes, which he enjoys who has a more delicate ear.[45]

---

42 Mersenne, *Harmonie universelle*, vol. III, p. 366.
43 See Appendix A.
44 1/136 of the just fifth is approximately 5.16 cents. One quarter of the syntonic comma is approximately 5.4 cents.
45 Mersenne, *Cogitata physico-mathematica*, p. 336.

This description is vivid, and strongly suggests that Mersenne may have learned first-hand about the actual setting of quarter-comma meantone temperament directly from Denis. In a subsequent paragraph, Mersenne provides a final clue as to the size of the diminishment of the fifth called for in Denis's *Traité*. As noted above, Denis states that the fifths in his temperament are to be diminished by '*un poinct*', a quantity that would seem to defy any attempt at precise definition. Yet shortly after the above description, Mersenne remarks that fifths are to be diminished:

. . . the quarter part of a comma, or as the practitioners say, diminished by a *puncto*.[46]

If Denis was indeed Mersenne's source for information about tuning procedure, it is not unreasonable to entertain the idea that *puncto* and *poinct* are equivalent and specific terms. It is not surprising that Denis made no attempt to be more explicit in his definition of the fifths' diminishment: he surely could not have done so in mathematical terms, nor in terms of any real precision. As a 'practitioner', Denis was interested not in commas or mathematics, but rather in a tuning that was 'harmonic' and resulted in an aural 'perfection' pleasing to the ear. Mersenne on the other hand, an author far more scientific in his approach to music theory, carried the issue further and precisely quantified the diminishment of the quarter-comma meantone fifth.

This argument cannot be closed without acknowledging a troublesome piece of evidence that might be summoned by the sceptic to refute the above conclusions. In the very same sentence where Denis mandates a diminishment of *un poinct* for the mean-tone fifths, he also makes the enigmatic statement that the *poinct* can be made 'as small as you would like' [*si petit que vous voudrez*] (p. 66). This puzzling pronouncement would appear to open the field yet again to the possibility of one-fifth or one-sixth comma meantone. Although fifths cannot be narrowed by much more than one-quarter of a comma without beating unpleasantly, Denis's statement would appear to allow diminishment by somewhat less than one-quarter of a comma.

This apparent prescription for license, however, is seemingly contradicted by the opening words of the same sentence. There, Denis

46 Mersenne, *Cogitata physico-mathematica*, p. 338.

says that the harpsichord is tuned 'to perfection (I say perfection because nothing can be added or diminished in this tuning without spoiling everything) . . . '. 'Perfection' implies one method, and one system. There cannot be two kinds of perfection. Nor can one diminish the fifths of meantone by less than one-quarter of a comma without 'spoiling' the 'perfection' of the major thirds and minor sixths. If there is any answer to the enigma, it is perhaps that Denis has made a momentary slip (it would not be the only one in the treatise), or that he is indulging in a penchant not uncommon among practitioners who discussed temperament: the cloaking of tuning methods in a certain amount of mystery.

Denis's unfortunate lack of ultimate specificity regarding his tuning system precludes unequivocal conclusions as to his meaning. It has not been possible, therefore, to construct a definitive proof. Nevertheless, the evidence offered here makes a clear case for Denis's advocacy of quarter-comma meantone temperament as the temperament of choice for his time and place. Part of his unwillingness to reveal all in print might indeed be laid to the traditional reluctance of the initiated to share their arcana. As Mersenne notes, the precise method of tuning keyboard instruments ' . . . is esteemed a great secret of the art by players',[47] an observation echoed many times by later theorists who take up the same subject.

Since the quarter-comma meantone system has played such an important role in this discussion, a brief review of its musical characteristics is in order. Contrary to a belief often encountered in print, quarter-comma meantone (in common with all regular temperaments including the other varieties of meantone) does *not* offer objectively differing key qualities. In regular temperaments, all intervals bearing the same name are the same size, no matter where they occur in the scale or on the keyboard. All the usable major triads in quarter-comma meantone are identical in terms of the sizes of their fifths and the sizes of their major and minor thirds; thus there is no objective difference in color between one tonality and another, and no sense of changing key-color is evident in the course of modulation. Theorists of the sixteenth and seventeenth centuries did indeed attach various affective characters to the different

---

47 Mersenne, *Harmonie universelle*, vol. III, p. 105.

modes,[48] but there is no acoustical basis in meantone temperament itself for such characterizations.

Nevertheless, the quarter-comma meantone system does offer a number of highly interesting features that helped to account for its remarkable longevity and popularity. The quarter-comma scale is very expressive melodically, for it contains semitones of unequal sizes (minor semitones of 76 cents and major semitones of 117.1 cents). Chromatic figures of all sorts, particularly the favored 'tetrachord' pattern of six consecutive notes within a fourth, were employed in the keyboard literature of the seventeenth century. Such coloristic figures were more common in the Italian and German keyboard repertoires than in the French, but French examples can also be found. The passages shown in Figures 1 and 2 gain greatly in interest and intensity when performed in quarter-comma meantone.

In terms of vertical sonorities, quarter-comma meantone temperament offers both pure intervals (major thirds and minor sixths) and intervals that are dissonant in varying degrees (such as the major seventh and diminished fourth). Composers, well aware of the resulting potential for color and contrast, were free to cultivate the judicious blending of pure sonorities, mild dissonances, and relatively more striking discordances. For example, in the keyboard literature of the seventeenth century, the diminished fourth (an interval 41.1 cents wider than the pure major third) was sometimes employed in cadences, where its unsettling presence served to further underscore the stability and repose of the subsequent tonic triad (Figure 3). The diminished fourth was also used as a melodic interval (Figure 4). At still other times, a dissonant interval like the diminished fourth seems to have been utilized purely for its exotic quality (Figure 5), even for its 'shock' value (Figure 6).

These and other opportunities for melodic expressiveness and dissonance/consonance contrast were actively exploited by composers of the sixteenth and seventeenth centuries; in a rare contemporary account, Louis Couperin's music is described by Jean Le Gallois as having been 'full of concords and enriched by fine

---

48 See, for example, Girolamo Diruta, *Il Transilvano* (Venice, 1593 [Part I] and 1609 [Part II]), Part II, Book IV, p. 22.

Figure 1 Jehan Titelouze, *Deposuit Potentes* (Alt. version). *Le Magnificat* (Paris, 1626), Guilmant/Pirro edition, p. 103, m. 16–24.

Figure 2 Louis Couperin, *Allemande. Pièces de clavecin*, Moroney edition No. 93, p. 144, m. 21–3.

Figure 3 Louis Couperin, *La Piémontaise. Pièces de clavecin*, Curtis edition No. 6, p. 15, m. 29–32.

Figure 4 Louis Couperin, *Sarabande en canon. Pièces de clavecin*, Moroney edition No. 47, p. 104, m. 20–2.

Figure 5 Louis Couperin, *Tombeau de Mr. de Blancrocher. Pièces de clavecin*, Moroney edition No. 81, p. 133, m. 45–7.

Figure 6 Louis Couperin, *Sarabande. Pièces de clavecin*, Moroney edition No. 51, p. 107, m. 1–3.

dissonances'.[49] Meantone temperament had much to do with the way such music was composed, played, and understood. Performed in a more recent temperament, a work intended for meantone presents an effect analogous to that conveyed by a black-and-white reproduction of an original oil painting: all the forms and outlines are apparent, but an entire layer of coloristic subtlety and meaning is missing.

49 Jean Le Gallois, 'Lettre de Monsieur Le Gallois à Mademoiselle Regnault de Solier touchant la musique' (Paris, 1680). The letter has been partially transcribed and translated by David Fuller in 'French harpsichord playing in the 17th century – *after Le Gallois*', *Early Music* iv (1976), pp. 22–6.

Unfortunately, there was a price to be paid for the advantages of quarter-comma meantone: on a standard keyboard with twelve notes per octave, it was possible at best to play in only nine of the major and minor keys (Bb, F, C, G, D, and A Major, and g, d, and a minor). The five accidentals on the keyboard were tuned as pure major thirds from natural keys, most often as C♯, Eb, F♯, G♯, and Bb. These were the chromatic notes customarily employed in sixteenth-century polyphony, and this arrangement generally sufficed as long as the practice of composition stayed within the bounds of the modal system. Yet there was no enharmonic equivalence, and inevitably there arose a demand for instruments that could both facilitate transposition and allow for the expansion of harmonic possibilities.

Keyboard instruments with more than twelve notes per octave have most often been dismissed in modern times as having been merely speculative (and generally unsuccessful) experiments. It should be recognized, however, that modifications of the standard twelve-note keyboard generally fell into two separate categories. The renowned *archicembalo* of Nicola Vicentino,[50] the *sambuca lincea* designed by Fabio Colonna and Scipione Stella,[51] and the complicated schemes presented by Mersenne, for keyboards with up to thirty-two notes per octave,[52] were indeed rather impractical attempts to provide for just intonation and/or intervals of the diatonic, chromatic, and enharmonic genera on keyboard instruments. Yet quite another tradition was developing at much the same time, involving far simpler arrangements that attempted to extend the usefulness of quarter-comma meantone through the provision of additional pure major thirds.

The most notable shortcoming of quarter-comma meantone temperament lay in the absence of the pitches D♯ and Ab. Without a D♯, a V–I cadence in the Phrygian mode was impossible. Without

50 For more on Nicola Vicentino and the *archicembalo*, see Vicentino, *L'antica musica ridotta alla moderna prattica* (Rome, 1555), Book V; Henry Kaufmann, *The life and works of Nicola Vicentino 1511–c. 1576* (Rome: American Institute of Musicology, 1966); and Kaufmann, 'More on the Tuning of the *Archicembalo*', *Journal of the American Musicological Society* xxiii (1970), 84–94.

51 For more information and additional bibliography concerning this instrument, see Lynn Martin, 'The Colonna-Stella *Sambuca lincea*, An Enharmonic Keyboard Instrument', *Journal of the American Musical Instrument Society* x (1984), pp. 5–21.

52 Mersenne, *Harmonie universelle*, vol. III, pp. 349–58.

an A♭, the Dorian mode could not be transposed to F.[53] These and other problems of similar nature are addressed by Jean Denis in the *Traité*. In response to such difficulties, a number of authors note the need for some sort of accommodation: either a compromise tuning of D♯/E♭ and G♯/A♭ so that these keys might serve for either note, or the addition of separate keys (and corresponding strings or pipes) for D♯ and A♭, so that two additional pure thirds might be added to the quarter-comma system without any alteration of the basic temperament. This inherently practical solution became quite popular in certain European countries, and was applied to organs, harpsichords, and clavichords. As we shall see, however, the procedure seems never to have found favor in France.

The practice of adding extra keys and pipes to organs is first documented in the 1480 contract for a new organ at the Church of San Martino, Lucca. Though the tuning used in that instrument cannot be identified with certainty, the contract did call for ' . . . the third above B-natural [D♯] and the minor third above F [A♭] together with their octaves where necessary'.[54] In the 1545 treatise *Lucidario in musica*, Pietro Aaron laments the fact that most Italian organs were still lacking such notes as D♯ and A♭, though later in the same treatise he does mention the existence of a split black key between G and A (to provide both G♯ and A♭) in certain '*organi moderni*'.[55] By the 1570s such split-key schemes had apparently become more popular in Italy, for Salinas writes that

. . . the Italians employ at least two dieses in every octave . . . the purpose being to provide a more common meeting ground between organist and choir. I have very often played on organs of this kind, especially on a very celebrated one at Florence, in the monastery of the Dominican brothers, called Santa Maria Novella.[56]

Later in his treatise there is further confirmation of the practice, and clear evidence that the temperament involved in these instances was quarter-comma meantone. Having stated that he finds this

---

53 The Dorian mode included a *mi-fa* major semitone between the second and third notes of its scale. In quarter-comma meantone, however, there was no *fa* at G♯; G–G♯ was a *minor* semitone, and was an unacceptable 41.1 cents narrower than the major semitone G–A♭.

54 Cited and translated by Mark Lindley in 'Fifteenth-Century Evidence for Meantone Temperament, *Proceedings of the Royal Musical Association* cii (1975–6), pp. 48–9. See also Luigi Nerici, *Storia della musica in Lucca* (Lucca, 1879), pp. 141–3.

55 Pietro Aaron, *Lucidario in musica* (Venice, 1545), pp. 35–6, 38.

56 Salinas, *De musica libri septem*, p. 81.

temperament superior to the one-third and two-sevenths comma systems, Salinas then furnishes detailed instructions to instrument builders for the application of the temperament. Invoking Euclid, he describes geometric divisions for the derivation of quarter-comma meantone and for its extension beyond twelve notes through the creation of additional pure thirds. Having derived the first twelve notes, he goes on as follows:

In this way instrument builders will be able to construct that diagram which they call 'diapason' . . . To these sounds of the diatonic and chromatic genera they will add at least two others of the enharmonic genus; these being, of course, A *molle* [A♭] and D raised enharmonic [D♯] . . . These two sounds will allow organists to match all the harmonies produced in choral music . . . Without these this is utterly impossible . . . But anyone desiring to obtain the [rest of the] enharmonic sounds can easily find them . . . always proceeding through major thirds.[57]

The difficulties of reconciling choir and organ discussed by Jean Denis in the *Traité* are directly related to the absence of D♯ and A♭.

Similar developments in keyboard design were under way in Northern Europe. At least one split-key arrangement was known to Arnolt Schlick, for he writes in 1511 that

. . . in the last twelve years an instrument was made that had double semitones in the manual and the pedal, so that if the commonly used semitones were too high or too low then the others with their special pipes and notes should be substituted, which one calls half-semitones or *ignoten*.[58]

As with the Lucca organ, we cannot be sure what sort of tuning was employed in the instrument to which Schlick refers. According to Schlick, the results in this particular instance were unsatisfactory, but the idea was not abandoned in Germany.

In the 1619 *De Organographia*, the first comprehensive treatise on the art of organbuilding, Michael Praetorius describes in detail many of the notable organs of his day, and along with their stoplists he provides highly specific information regarding their keyboard arrangements. Several of these instruments include additional split accidentals (called 'subsemitones' by Praetorius) in manuals and pedal, providing for a D♯ (at the Schöningen Schlosskapelle, for

57 Salinas, *De musica libri septem*, pp. 158–60. The most important passages from this section have been translated by Arthur Daniels in 'Microtonality and Mean-Tone Temperament', *Journal of Music Theory* ix (1965), pp. 268–73. Daniels's translations quoted here.
58 Schlick, *Spiegel der Orgelmacher und Organisten*, p. 77. trans. E. Barber.

example) or for both D♯ and A♭ (Bückeburg Stadtkirche and Dresden Schlosskapelle).[59] Such instruments were also built in Weimar, Bayreuth, Hamburg, Braunschweig, Wolfenbüttel, and numerous other locations in northern and central Germany.[60] For the most part, these instruments were located in the more important churches or court chapels, where renowned 'professional' players served. Many of the most important composers of the North German organ school, including Samuel Scheidt, Michael Praetorius, and Jacob Praetorius, had such instruments at their disposal. They wrote numerous works that took advantage of the enhanced possibilities, and D♯s appear with particular frequency in these compositions. The organs of smaller towns and village churches had, for the most part, only the customary twelve notes per octave. For such instruments, tuned as they would have been in quarter-comma meantone, Praetorius suggests a compromise value for G♯–A♭.[61]

Elsewhere in the *De Organographia*, in the chapter on the '*Clavicymbalum Universale, seu perfectum*', Praetorius comments further on the need for split accidentals, for both organs and harpsichords. It is clear from the references to the desirability of pure major thirds that quarter-comma meantone is the temperament he has in mind.

The harpsichord . . . and the like, otherwise called *Instrumenta* (though incorrectly, as mentioned before), are rather incomplete and imperfect in that they do not afford chromatic tones such as can be produced on lutes and viols da gamba. On this account various harpsichords, in accordance with the specifications of good organists, have been provided with two different keys for the D♯, such that in the Aeolian mode transposed a fourth lower, the third falling between the B and F♯' may be had in a pure and correct form.

In my modest opinion, it would be very advisable to make double keys for the D♯ and also the G♯ on the positive and organ as well as on the harpsichord. (This is even more necessary for the organ than for the harpsichord, the strings of which can easily be retuned and adjusted). Thus in the Hypodorian mode transposed a second lower to F, one would be able to obtain the minor third above the F quite justly and purely[62] from the A♭ key which would be made

59 Praetorius, *Syntagma Musicum*, vol. II, pp. 185–8.
60 Hans Koltz, *Über die Orgelkunst der Gotik, der Renaissance und des Barock* (Kassel: Bärenreiter, 1975), pp. 215–26.
61 Praetorius, *Syntagma Musicum*, vol. II, p. 155. To modern ears, this compromise is far from entirely satisfactory.
62 This is a slip; the author surely meant only to refer to the normal minor third of meantone temperament, 6 cents smaller than pure.

next to the G♯; and one might well have many more variations of this kind in the chromatic genus.[63]

Both the quarter-comma meantone temperament prescribed by Praetorius and the use of subsemitones persisted in Germany and in other European countries through the end of the seventeenth century and beyond. Andreas Werckmeister, in the 1698 edition of the *Orgel-Probe*, makes reference to keyboards with 'the conventional three or more subsemitones',[64] though he characterizes such keyboards as 'patched up and spoiled'.[65] Subsemitones had appeared on Spanish organs in the sixteenth and seventeenth centuries,[66] and were also known in seventeenth-century England. Two noted instruments built in London during the 1680s by Father Smith, at the Temple Church and at Durham Cathedral, were equipped with subsemitones.[67] During the eighteenth century, the organ played by Handel at the Foundling Hospital was designed with a sixteen-note octave, but incorporated an apparently unique system that did not make use of divided accidentals. Instead, C♯, E♭, G♯ and B♭ could be changed to their respective enharmonic counterparts by moving stop-knobs at either side of the keyboard. Unfortunately, the player was forced to choose between having either the normal accidentals or their respective enharmonic counterparts; no mix of the two groups was possible.[68]

As mentioned above, split keys were also employed in harpsichords. Perhaps the first clear and unambiguous reference to the practice is made by Juan Bermudo in the 1555 *Libro llamado declaración de instrumentos musicales*.

I presuppose as a certainty that the black key between G and A was formerly *fa* but now serves as *mi* [although] in some harpsichords from Flanders the said key occurs in a way that forms both *fa* and *mi* . . . [69]

63 Praetorius, *Syntagma Musicum*, vol. II, pp. 63–4 (trans. Harold Blumenfeld).
64 Werckmeister, *Orgel-Probe*, p. 68 (trans. Krapf).
65 Werckmeister, *Orgel-Probe*, p. 66 (trans. Krapf). As the enthusiastic proponent of new tuning systems, Werckmeister had his own particular reasons for offering this assessment.
66 See Klotz, *Über die Orgelkunst*, p. 140, and Peter Williams, *The European Organ* (London: Batsford, 1966), p. 251.
67 Peter Williams, 'Equal Temperament and the English Organ, 1675–1825', *Acta Musicologica* xl (1968), p. 57.
68 Williams, 'Equal Temperament', pp. 62–3.
69 Juan Bermudo, *Libro llamado declaración de instrumentos musicales* (Osuna, 1555), fol. 104ᵛ; cited and translated by Mark Lindley in *Lutes, Viols and Temperaments*

Jean Denis and meantone temperament

Harpsichords with auxiliary accidentals became particularly popular in Italy, and Frescobaldi is known to have had access to many such instruments during his career.[70] A number of Italian harpsichords so constructed have survived with their original keyboards, and it has been suggested that other surviving antiques were also originally equipped with split accidentals which disappeared when keyboards were replaced during subsequent alterations.[71] Nevertheless, the practice of adding additional keys in each octave never seems to have become as popular in harpsichords as in organs. This can probably be attributed, in part at least, to the difficulties of fitting extra strings and jacks into an already-narrow octave span that barely allowed sufficient clearance for twelve jacks to function, let alone fourteen or more.

The above references to split accidentals have been reviewed in some detail in order to underscore the comparative paucity of evidence for similar arrangements in France, particularly for the simpler schemes that extended the meantone octave with one or two additional chromatic notes. Mersenne does indeed refer several times to the potential benefits of adding keys beyond the normal number (though he notes that the ancients 'banished those who added new strings to instruments').[72] The majority of his comments and illustrations, however, refer to more complicated keyboard systems that attempt to provide for some form of just intonation. In one of these instances it is plainly evident that he is referring to instruments of Italian manufacture.[73] In other cases, it is never clear

(Cambridge: Cambridge University Press, 1984), pp. 16–17. In Book I of the *Musica practica* (Bologna, 1482), Ramos de Pareja does make brief mention of divided accidental keys, but it appears likely that he was referring only to the clavichord, not to the harpsichord or organ. See Standley Howell, 'Ramos de Pareja's "Brief Discussion of Various Instruments"', *Journal of the American Musical Instrument Society* xi (1985), pp. 24–5 and Lindley, 'Fifteenth-Century Evidence', pp. 48–9.

70 See Frederick Hammond, *Girolamo Frescobaldi* (Cambridge, Mass.: Harvard University Press, 1983), pp. 103–7. This information should give pause to those who would conclude that keyboard works by Frescobaldi, Froberger, *et al.* containing *both* accidentals of an enharmonic pair (D♯/E♭, for example) were of necessity conceived for some temperament other than meantone.

71 See John Barnes, 'The Specious Uniformity of Italian Harpsichords', in *Keyboard Instruments: Studies in Keyboard Organology*, ed. Edwin Ripin (Edinburgh: Edinburgh University Press, 1971; reprint edition, New York: Dover Publications, 1977), pp. 1–10.

72 Mersenne, *Harmonie universelle*, vol. III, p. 353.

73 ' . . . harpsichords can be made that have all their tones divided into four parts, in order to make the enharmonic dieses everywhere . . . It has been written to me from Rome that Mr. Jean Baptiste de Bonis of Cortone, a town in Tuscany, has made excellent ones, which

41

whether he is describing his own speculative designs, actual innovations of French builders, or experiments from other countries about which he has heard. Thus, when he reports that complicated keyboards 'can be played as easily as the others when the hands have become accustomed to them',[74] we cannot be sure whether he is speaking from experience or merely speculating about what might be possible.

In only one place does Mersenne describe a keyboard modification that sounds like a straightforward extension of the meantone octave. Regarding the note G♯, he remarks that

> ... this last *feinte* has no fifth above it. This is why the makers of harpsichords call this fifth the *deffaut de l'accord*. Thus it happens that some cut it in two in order to find the fifth in this location, through which the imperfection of the temperament is evaded.[75]

The 'some' who made this modification, however, are not identified as French builders.

Nowhere in his treatise does Denis refer to the use of split accidentals in his own day, either for organs or harpsichords. Surviving French harpsichords of the seventeenth century show no evidence of the practice,[76] and at least one theorist further corroborates this apparent lack. In the *Traité de la viole* of 1687, Jean Rousseau explains the difference between the major and minor semitones, and continues as follows.

> The difference between these two semitones is apparent on the monochord, and we are aware of the necessity for distinguishing them through the *Clavecins coupez*, or with split accidentals, that the Italians use. Nevertheless,

---

have all their keys broken or cut and which can be tuned with admirable ease in all the ways that could be imagined.' (*Harmonie universelle*, vol. III, pp. 215–16). A 1617 virginal by Bonis, with a more conventional and practical arrangement of split keys, is illustrated in Hammond, *Girolamo Frescobaldi*, pp. 108–9.

74 Mersenne, *Harmonie universelle*, vol. III, p. 354.

75 Mersenne, *Harmonie universelle*, vol. III, p. 365.

76 Conversation with William Dowd. Only two very late French harpsichords are known to have been constructed with auxiliary keys. In his *Essai sur la musique ancienne et moderne* (Paris, 1780, pp. 344–5), Jean-Benjamin de Laborde denounces equal temperament as a 'vice' and calls for a system of just intonation, to be applied on a harpsichord with 21 notes per octave. Such an instrument, the single-strung *clavecin chromatique*, was apparently built for him in 1781 by Jacques Goermanns of Paris. For more on the *clavecin chromatique*, see Pierre-Joseph Roussier, *Mémoire sur le nouveau clavecin chromatique de M. de Laborde* (Paris, 1782). According to Laborde, another harpsichord with split sharps belonged to Christophe Chiquelier, *Garde des Instruments de la Musique du Roi*; this instrument had been constructed by Pascal Taskin. See Laborde, *Essai*, vol. I, p. 345.

this is not done at all in France, which often causes unfortunate results in transposed *tons*, in which the cadences that are made on accidentals are not always in tune, especially on the harpsichord.[77]

Why the seventeenth-century French harpsichord builders appear to have shunned the use of auxiliary accidentals remains a mystery. It might be tempting to further conclude that the arrangement was unknown in French organs, but the phrase must be amended to 'almost unknown'. The contract for at least one major Paris organ, at St-Nicolas-des-Champs (Crespin Carlier, 1632–6), called for split sharps for D♯/E♭ in three octaves of both *Grand-Orgue* and *Positif* divisions.[78] There is doubt, however, as to whether the instrument was in fact so constructed.[79] Denis's rules for transpositions to avoid the need for nonexistent D♯s and A♭s were obviously directed to the great majority of organists who did not have subsemitones available to them.

In closing, a last observation relating to organs and meantone tuning should be made. It has long been accepted as a commonplace that stringed instruments tuned in meantone could have been quickly and easily retuned to provide for alternative accidentals, but that large church organs offered no such flexibility. This assertion is only partially correct. If an organist desired to use a D♯ or an A♭ during a particular part of the service, and was willing to play that section on one of the reed stops of the organ, the adjustment could easily have been made. The reed pipes were located in the most accessible places on the chest or chests, for these were the pipes whose tuning required constant attention. In fact, the organist and an assistant (who held down keys as needed) would have retuned the reed pipes before every important use of the organ. The tuning of such pipes involves no change in their length, but only a change in the length of the flexible brass reed-tongue, effected by a simple adjustment of the sliding tuning wire.

---

77 Jean Rousseau, *Traité de la viole* (Paris, 1687), p. 50.
78 See Klotz, *Über die Orgelkunst*, p. 190.
79 See Pierre Hardouin, 'La composition des orgues que pouvaient toucher les musiciens parisiens aux alentours de 1600', in *La musique instrumentale de la Renaissance* (Paris: Éditions du Centre National de la Recherche Scientifique, 1955), p. 268, n. 19.

# 3

# The eight *tons* of the church

In the chapter entitled '*Des huict Tons de l'Église*' (pp. 84–7), Denis turns his attention to certain problems related to the use of the organ in Gallican rite. These difficulties arose out of the practice of alternation between organ and choir during parts of the liturgy, a convention by then well established in France. The organ's interpolated sections, called versets, replaced sung plainsong portions of the Mass ordinary and proper, psalms, canticles, and hymns.

The first documentary evidence of ecclesiastical permission for alternation in France dates from 1510,[1] although there are indications that *alternatim* practices of various kinds had become customary long before that.[2] The first French keyboard versets to appear in print were contained in two volumes issued in 1530 and 1531 in Paris by Pierre Attaingnant, the *Magnificat sur les huit tons avec Te deum laudamus et deux preludes* and the *Tablature pour le jeu dorgues espinetes et manicordions sur le plain chant de Cunctipotens et Kyrie fons*. The versets in the Attaingnant volumes are characterized by technical simplicity and close correspondence to the plainsong melodies.

After the Attaingnant prints, there followed a gap of more than ninety years until the appearance of the next surviving printed collections of organ versets, the *Hymnes de l'Eglise pour toucher sur l'orgue, avec les fugues et recherches sur leur plain-chant* (Paris: Pierre Ballard, 1623) and *Le Magnificat, ou cantique de la Vierge pour toucher sur l'orgue, suivant les huit tons de l'Eglise* (Paris: Pierre Ballard, 1626) of Jehan Titelouze. In the preface to the initial volume, Titelouze avers that these are the first volumes of such music to have been published within anyone's recollection.

Like the pieces in the Attaingnant prints, the predominantly con-

---

1 See Yvonne Rokseth, Introduction to *Deux livres d'orgue* (Paris: Attaingnant, 1530 and 1531; modern edition, Paris: Heugel, 1967), p. xii.
2 Benjamin Van Wye, 'Ritual Use of the Organ in France', *Journal of the American Musicological Society* xxxiii (1980), pp. 287–90.

servative versets of Titelouze are largely derived from the corresponding plainsong. In his skillful employment of learned contrapuntal devices and motet-like textures largely derived from sixteenth-century vocal models, Titelouze shows himself to be a keeper of Renaissance tradition rather than an innovator (though there are occasional exceptions, as in the example on p. 33). The settings in the two volumes were presumably not intended for the highly accomplished 'professional' organist, who would likely have improvised most of the required versets directly from the plainchant melodies of the choir book.[3] The *Magnificat* collection in particular seems to have been intended for students and others (including provincial organists) of modest ability, as may be judged from the following passage in the Introduction to the volume:

Note also that, having realized that my *Hymnes* were deemed too difficult for those needing instruction (since it is for them that I have produced this volume), I have reduced as much as I could the amount of facility required, and have taken it upon myself to bring the parts closer together, so that they can be played with less difficulty.

The ceremonial handbooks of Jean Denis's time cover the use of alternation in some detail, and it is clear that in Paris at least, the practice was well established by the middle years of the seventeenth century. The *Caeremoniale Parisiense* of Martin Sonnet (Paris, 1662), though forbidding employment of the organ during the penitential seasons of Lent and Advent, sanctions the use of the instrument in Matins, Lauds, First and Second Vespers, Terce, Compline, Salut, and Station after Vespers, as well as in all parts of the Mass ordinary except the Credo. The organ was to give the first verset or intonation of all other parts of the ordinary except the Gloria, and could also participate in the performance of hymns and certain sections of the proper.[4]

3 Organists competing for posts at prominent French churches in the sixteenth and seventeenth centuries would almost certainly have been required to demonstrate proficiency in improvisation as a prerequisite for employment. Indeed, Titelouze's success in obtaining his post at the Rouen Cathedral in 1588 was due in part to the fact that he was 'markedly superior to the other candidates in improvisational skill' (see Almonte Howell, 'Titelouze', *The New Grove*, vol. xix, pp. 13–14). If unusual reliance upon improvisatory expertise in the *alternatim* context was, in fact, the norm for French organists until the later seventeenth century, therein lies a possible explanation for the puzzling scarcity of printed French liturgical organ repertory dating from that time.

4 Cited by Edward Higginbottom in 'French Classical Organ Music and the Liturgy', *Proceedings of the Royal Musical Association* ciii (1976–7), pp. 23–9. See also Higgin-

This enhanced liturgical role for the organ helped to inspire the numerous printed collections of organ versets that were published in Paris in the later seventeenth and early eighteenth centuries, including the *livres d'orgue* of Guillaume-Gabriel Nivers, Nicolas Lebègue, André Raison, and Jacques Boyvin. A distinct evolution is discernible from the versets of Titelouze to those of the later composers, an evolution marked by rapidly diminishing dependence on plainchant as a compositional underpinning and ever-increasing secularization of forms and motifs. By 1700, many of the versets heard in Paris churches were related only by pitch-level to the plainsong verses they replaced.

Next it must be recognized that when Denis speaks of the eight '*tons* sung in the church (which the organist should know)' (p. 84), he is referring to a convention that goes beyond what is implied by concept of 'modes' or by the term 'psalm tones'. For Denis and the other French organists of his time, the *tons* were practical devices of pitch determination, designed to aid the organist in coordinating the chant of the antiphons, the psalm tones of the psalms themselves, and the pitch level of the organ music. The organist not only had to play his versets at appropriate pitches, but also had to end the versets in specific ways in order to help the choir find its pitch for the succeeding verse. In addition, the choir's recitation pitches needed to be located in a range comfortable for the singers, which meant that various transpositions were required. In such a situation there existed considerable potential for confusion. By thinking in terms of a *ton*, which implied a specific pitch level and location on the keyboard, and a specific relationship between dominant and final, the organist was able to adapt a relatively small number of formulas to cover a large and varied assortment of practical situations, even instances in which a psalm tone and the mode of a given antiphon were in conflict.[5]

Of all extant sources, the *Dissertation sur le chant grégorien* of Guillaume-Gabriel Nivers (Paris, 1683) offers the most comprehen-

bottom, 'Ecclesiastical Prescription and Musical Style in French Classical Organ Music', *The Organ Yearbook* xii (1981), pp. 31–54, and Norbert Dufourcq, 'De l'emploi du temps des organistes Parisiens sous les régnes de Louis XIII et Louis XIV', *La Revue Musicale* ccxxvi (1955), pp. 35–47.

5 Such situations are discussed by Pierre Maillart in *Les tons, ou discours, sur les modes de musique et les tons de l'église* (Tournai, 1610), pp. 268–72.

sive discussion of the relationship of the organ's interpolations to the sung plainsong of the choir. In this passage Nivers further explains the role of the organ in setting the choir's pitches.

> . . . in churches where the organ is used in the divine service, it is a rule of absolute necessity that the organ should give the *ton* of everything that is sung after the organ by the choir. The first [organ] antiphon must therefore be at the *ton* of the second which is sung by the choir immediately after the organ has played the first, and so on for the others. That is why the singers, without submitting themselves to the bother of rules, need only pay attention to the final of the organ (and nothing beyond that, since the attempt to find the *ton* while the organ is playing is ever one of the principal causes of discord and error), and on this final of the organ, which should always be the final of the antiphon which is to be intoned, [they can] regulate by proportion the first note of the antiphon.[6]

Some idea of the concept of *ton* and its practical function for the organist may be obtained by substituting 'pitch' or 'pitch level' for the word *ton* in the above excerpt. The organ did not necessarily give the exact pitch upon which the choir was to begin, but *did* give the final of the antiphon in question, from which the singers could then find their beginning pitch. At least one writer has been tempted to suggest the term 'key' as an equivalent for *ton*.[7] Though such a notion cannot be pursued very far without breaking down, the fundamental idea of 'key' can help to clarify the concept of *ton* as understood by the organist.

Denis's *tons*, as may be noted in Table 3, do not always follow the orthodox dominants and finals of the plainsong tones. As is stated numerous times in the *Traité*, several were regularly transposed up or down 'for the convenience of the choir'. The necessity for such transpositions arose because of the uncomfortably wide range of dominants in the traditional plainsong tones. In Table 3, in the column 'Common psalm tones', it will be noted that the dominants of the untransposed tones fall within the span of f to d', a range far too wide to have been comfortable for all the voices in a choir. Nivers amplifies the point in this way:

---

6 Guillaume-Gabriel Nivers, *Dissertation sur le chant grégorien* (Paris, 1683), p. 111.
7 Almonte Howell, 'French Baroque Organ Music and the Eight Church Tones', *Journal of the American Musicological Society* xi (1959), pp. 110–13 and *passim*. See also the use of the term 'pitch-key mode' in Walter Atcherson, 'Key and Mode in Seventeenth-Century Music Theory Books', *Journal of Music Theory* xvii (1973), pp. 216–22.

Table 3 *Finals and dominants of the* tons *according to
Denis and Nivers*

| | Common psalm tones[a] | Ambitus of corresponding mode | Denis (*Traité*) 1650 | Nivers (*Dissertation*) 1683 | Ambitus of corresponding mode |
|------|------|------|------|------|------|
| I | d–a | d–d′ | d–a | d–a | d–d′ |
| II | d–f | A–a | g–b♭ | g–b♭ | d–d′ |
| III | e–c′ | e–e′ | f–b♭, e–c′ | g–b♭ | f–f′ (e–e′, g–g′) |
| IV | e–a | B–b | e–a | e–a | B–b |
| V | f–c′ | f–f′ | c–g | c–g, d–a | c–c′ (d–d′) |
| VI | f–a | c–c′ | f–a | f–a | c–c′ |
| VII | g–d′ | g–g′ | c–g | c–g, d–a | c–c′ (d–d′) |
| VIII | g–c′ | d–d′ | f–b♭ | f–b♭ | c–c′ |
| | Range of dominants: f–d′ | Total range of system: A–g′ | Range of dominants: g–b♭ | Range of dominants: g–b♭ | Total range of system: B–f′ (g′) |

[a]These were the common psalm tones as specified by the following seventeenth-century theorists, among others: Pierre Maillart (*Les tons* [Tournai, 1610], pp. 212–13), Adriano Banchieri (*Cartella musicale* [Venice, 1614], pp. 68–9), Antoine Parran (*Traité de la musique* [Paris, 1639], p. 113), Denis (p. 84), and Nivers (*Dissertation*, p. 107).

Each *ton* has two essential notes, called the final and the dominant, on which all the sorts of chants are based . . . The final is the note on which one should most often begin, and always end. The dominant is the note which most often dominates the chant, and upon which the tenor of the psalms is sung . . . That is why this dominant should be a bit higher than the middle of the natural voice, and not lower, because in all the *tons* the range of the notes is greater below the dominants than above.[8]

Denis's solution (or rather, the current practice he reports) involves transpositions of *tons* II, III, V, VII, and VIII. As Table 3 shows, these transpositions result in a considerable compression of the range of the dominants: two are now on g, three on a, and three on b♭. In addition, the ambitus of the entire system for the singers was reduced from the nearly two octaves of A–g′ to B–f′.[9] Trans-

8 Nivers, *Dissertation*, pp. 105–6.
9 In 1605 and again in 1614, Adriano Banchieri had set forth a very similar system of transpositions designed to facilitate 'the alternation of plainchant and organ', though he noted that these transpositions could 'generate confusion amongst singers and organists not well accomplished in their professions'. See Banchieri, *L'organo suonarino* (Venice,

positions also allowed choir and organist to cope more easily with situations in which subsequent antiphons were in different *tons*, a difficulty addressed by Nivers.[10]

Transposing some of the *tons* in order to place the dominants of all eight on the same note might have seemed an even more attractive solution. Though Denis does not directly explain why this was inadvisable, Nivers does address the subject.

> . . . to continue and pass immediately to other pieces on different *tons* in the same Office, the different dominants must not always be regulated to the same note . . . For to say that the same dominant must always be kept by the choir is a universal error, the certain cause and undoubted source of nearly all the disorders and confusions in the chant that is heard each day in our churches.[11]

There are certain *tons*, he continues, which, if they are sung one after the other with the same dominants, 'have such a strong antipathy that nature itself cannot bear them'.[12]

The truth of this is well illustrated in the *Dictionaire de musique* of Sébastien de Brossard (Paris, 1705). On page 212, the eight *tons* are shown with the signatures required for them to share a common dominant on a. For *tons* I, IV, and VI, no transposition is required, and the transpositions for *tons* V and VII present no problems. *Ton* II, however, has been transposed to f♯, *ton* III to c♯, and *ton* VIII to e. It is hard to imagine how such awkward transpositions would, as Brossard claims, have afforded '*beaucoup de facilité*'.[13]

Unusual transpositions were made even less workable in Denis's time by the fact that the organ was likely to have been tuned in quarter-comma meantone, which meant that enharmonic notes such as D♯ and A♭ were lacking. Thus follow Denis's warnings that the organist must avoid certain transpositions that the choirmaster might request, and that organist and choirmaster must come to agreement regarding pitches (p. 76). That this did not always

---

1605), pp. 39–44, and *Cartella musicale* (Venice, 1614), pp. 71, 88. For further evidence of such transpositions in early seventeenth-century Italy, see *La regola del contraponto e della musical compositione* of Camillo Angleria (Milan, 1622), pp. 80–5. Another discussion of transposition in the liturgical context appears in Diruta, *Il Transilvano*, Part II (Venice, 1609), Book III.

10 Nivers, *Dissertation*, pp. 110–12.
11 Nivers, *Dissertation*, p. 109.
12 Nivers, *Dissertation*, p. 109.
13 Sébastien de Brossard, *Dictionaire de musique* (Paris, 1705), p. 212.

happen is suggested by the references of Nivers to 'discords and cacophonies that occur all too often' in churches.[14]

Table 3 also shows that the transpositions set out by Nivers correspond rather closely to those Denis had published, which has brought a suggestion that Denis must have been Nivers's disciple in the matter.[15] This notion must be discounted, however, for at the time of publication of Denis's *Traité* (1650 edition), Nivers was but eighteen years of age. It is not inconceivable that Nivers was in fact Denis's disciple, and at the very least the statements of both men appear to reflect a common, well-established practice.

---

14 Nivers, *Dissertation*, p. 109. For more on such confusions, see the interesting comments of Michael Praetorius in the prefatory pages to vol. II of the *Syntagma Musicum* (pp. xi–xii).
15 Almonte Howell, 'French Baroque Organ Music', p. 113.

# 4

# Notes on the translation

Jean Denis was clearly not a man of letters, and the language and syntax of the *Traité de l'accord de l'espinette* are frequently problematical, far more so than in other French musical treatises of the period. Sentences amble on at great length, often changing tense and subject along the way. Misprints, errors of grammar, and tangled constructions abound.

Topics in the *Traité* frequently change without the appearance of a new paragraph, resulting in blocks of text that sometimes extend unbroken for several pages. For the sake of clarity, these long units have been broken down into paragraphs of more reasonable length. Similarly, exceptionally long sentences have generally been broken down into shorter ones, without (it is hoped) compromising their sense. Obvious typographical errors have been corrected and translated without comment. Archaic punctuation has been modernized, and quotation marks and parentheses have been added where they are clearly called for by the context. Occasional editorial insertions in the text are enclosed in square brackets.

Throughout the entire translation, the word *espinette* has been translated as 'harpsichord' rather than 'spinet'.[1] In numerous French sources of the seventeenth century (such as the inventories of builders' shops), the terms *espinette* [spinet] and *clavecin* [harpsichord] are employed in contexts that clearly suggest a distinction between the two instruments. Nevertheless, the French also tended to use the word *espinette* in a general way to refer to all quilled instruments, much as the English employed the word 'virginal'. For example, Chambonnières appears in royal payment records as *joueur d'espinette*, though he surely played harpsichords as well as spinets. In a letter of 6 April 1655 to the Paris organist Henri Du Mont, Constantin Huygens writes:

---

1 The only exceptions come in the Sestina and Sonnet at the beginning of the treatise; 'harpsichord' could not be made to fit the meter.

... I have learned through letters from Anvers that the celebrated Couchet[2] has died there, which is a sad loss to amateurs interested in good *espinettes*. I would be glad to have one of Couchet's with two keyboards, like that of M. de Chambonnières, which was quite excellent ... [3]

Mersenne and Pierre Trichet mention double, triple, and quadruple *espinettes* that possess several stops controlled by sliding registers, references that suggest instruments beyond those ordinarily associated with the term 'spinet'.[4] Later in the century, in the *Dictionnaire universel* (The Hague and Rotterdam, 1690), Antoine Furetière states that the *clavecin* is 'a type of *espinette*', and in the eighteenth century this usage continued. In the article on the harpsichord from the *Encyclopédie méthodique* (Paris, 1785) is found the following:

Ordinary spinets [*epinettes ordinaires*] were six feet long and two and one-half feet wide. They have two keyboards. The upper has one jack on each key. The lower keyboard has two jacks on each key; one plucks a string at eight-foot pitch, the other plucks a string at four-foot pitch ... The best makers of ordinary spinets have been the Ruckers, at Antwerp ... and Jean Denis of Paris.[5]

Thus the word *espinette* possessed a generic as well as a specific meaning. Throughout the *Traité*, and particularly in such phrases as 'the *espinette* is the most perfect instrument of all instruments' (p. 64), Denis appears to be using the term *espinette* in its general sense as 'harpsichord', and the word has been so translated here.

The word *feinte* also represents a dilemma for the translator. There is no satisfactory English equivalent for this term, though it is clear that *feintes* most often refers, in this and other treatises, to the raised keys of the keyboard. In the original sense of the word, *feintes* were the notes of *musica ficta* (feigned music), notes outside the traditional hexachord system; French treatises of the sixteenth cen-

2 Joannes Couchet (ca. 1612–55), grandson of Hans Ruckers, took over the Antwerp shop of the Ruckers family in 1642 and carried on its tradition of excellence in the building of stringed keyboard instruments.
3 W. J. A. Jonckbloet and J. P. N. Land, eds., *Musique et musiciens au XVIIᵉ siècle: Correspondance et oeuvres musicales de Constantin Huygens* (Leyden: E. J. Brill, 1882), p. 24.
4 Mersenne, *Harmonie universelle*, vol. III, p. 106, and Pierre Trichet, *Traité des instruments de musique* (ca. 1640), p. 172.
5 *Encyclopédie méthodique* (Paris, 1785), vol. iv (*Instruments de musique*). Cited and translated by Hubbard in *Three Centuries of Harpsichord Making*, p. 255.

tury refer to such notes as *chant feint*.[6] Strictly speaking, a *feinte* was in fact a *fa feint*, a new note that was a *mi–fa* major semitone higher than an existing diatonic note. Thus, as Denis explains, the *feinte* E♭ has its own solmization syllable, *fa* (p. 61).

By the time of Denis's treatise, however, the term *feintes* had come to refer to *all* the raised keys of the keyboard, whether or not such notes were actually a major semitone higher than the notes below them; thus C♯, for example, a *minor* semitone above C, is termed a *feinte* by Denis. Also employed by Denis are the newer terms *dieses* [sharps] and *bémols* [flats]. These expressions lead to confusion when used alongside the term *feinte*, and Denis stumbles badly when he tries to explain how *dieses* differ from *feintes* (see p. 69, and n. 35 to the translation).

6 See Blockland de Montfort, *Instruction méthodique et fort facile pour apprendre la musique practique* (Lyons, 1587), p. 48, and Jean Yssandon, *Traité de la musique pratique* (Paris, 1582), p. 7.

# TREATISE ON THE TUNING
## OF THE HARPSICHORD

With a Comparison of its Keyboard
to Vocal Music.

*Augmented in this Edition by the Following Four
Chapters.*

I.   Treatise on Sounds and the Number Thereof.
II.  Treatise on the *tons* of the Church and their Ranges.
III. Treatise on Fugues and How They Should be Realized.
IV.  The Proper Manner of Playing the Harpsichord and the
Organ.

*Dedicated to*
My Lord
THE MARQUIS OF MORTEMART.

By J. DENIS, *Organist of Saint-Barthélemy, and Master
Builder of Musical Instruments.*

IN PARIS.

By ROBERT BALLARD, Sole Music Printer
to the King.
And for Sale at the home of the Author, rue des Arcis
at the Image of Saint Cecilia.

———

M. DC. L.

# SESTINA

The little book now in your hand
The spinet-tuner's art doth tell,
Regals and Trumpets, Flutes as well.
Obedient to the Lord's command,
To serve Him here and far abroad,
I've dedicated it to God.

Some readers are properly humble
While others would love to undo me.
It's easy to show where I stumble,
But harder indeed to outdo me.
R.[1]

---

1 Honorat Racan (1589–1670) and Mathurin Régnier (1573–1613) are possible candidates for authorship of this epigram.

# Epistle

TO MY LORD

## THE MARQUIS OF MORTEMART,[2]

### ADVISOR TO THE KING
### IN HIS PUBLIC AND PRIVATE COUNCILS,

Knight of the Orders of His Majesty, First Gentleman of the Chamber, Bailiff and Captain of the Hunting Preserve of the Louvre, the Chateau of Madrid, the Park and Forest of Boulogne, La Muette[3] and St-Cloud, with the Right of Jurisdiction over the said locales, and Captain of the Chaillot Hunt.

MY LORD,

Among all the splendid talents which embellish your illustrious person and which you possess to perfection, I may say that music, both theoretical and practical, is the one you place above all others. It is for just cause that you should be called the father of this science, for it is instilled in you so deeply and you practice it so naturally that you are without equal. No one else can so skillfully unite his voice with the lute, or the theorbo, or whatever instrument it pleases you to take up, for you are marvelously well versed in the most melodious among them.

So many times have I had the honor of joining the company of your admirers when you were engaged in this agreeable diversion that I must declare, along with them, that I have never heard anything so sweet, nor so ravishing, and that in music, as in every other thing, your spirit is incomparable and your skill inimitable. Thus,

---

2 For more on the Marquis de Mortemart, see the Introduction, pp. 12–13.

3 The hunting lodge on this site, named for the *mues* (antlers) brought there as trophies or the *mue* (moulting) of falcons and hawks, was later replaced by a small château, which stood north of today's Chaussée de la Muette in Paris (16ᵉ Arrondissement).

57

words other than my own are needed to celebrate your glory, which is already so well known among the neighboring nations that anything that could be said of it would only repeat what has already been said, which even so hardly approaches the reality I have so often known and so agreeably heard.

For this reason, my lord, I have been so bold as to present to you this modest treatise on harpsichord tuning, as a due recognition of all your perfections. If you deign to consider and kindly receive this humble work, which represents but a fragment of all the knowledge you possess so completely, then I shall indeed dare to hope that your name will win it entry into the best households, and that with your approbation it will there be gladly received, coming as it does from the hand of him who is proud to be,

MY LORD,
Your most humble and
most obedient servant,
J. DENIS

# On the subject of harpsichord tuning

SONNET

A scheme that perfect harmony will bring,
You say, Denis, that you to us would show.
For proper playing we must tune high and low,
The organ's pipes and all the spinet's strings.

And showing perfect knowledge of these things,
You say the tones must rise that now are low,
The high ones fall – in Nature 'tis not so.[4]
Will you advise, and guide our wanderings?

A tuner needs a keen, discerning ear,
A boon from Mother Nature seldom won.
You know this well, of doubt there can be none.

Of such exalted marvels have no fear,
But fifths a bit diminished bear in mind,
And perfect concord you will surely find.

                                        J. D. L. J.[5]

4 This paradox is apparently a reference to Denis's procedure for setting meantone temperament. According to his temperament instructions (p. 71), the lower notes of fifths are raised in pitch, or the upper notes lowered, in order to create the requisite narrowed fifths.
5 *Jean Denis Le Jeune*, this to distinguish Denis from his father of the same name (1549–after 1634).

## TABLE
### OR PERFECT SYSTEM FOR MEASURING ALL THE INTERVALS AND CONSONANCES
of the keyboard of the harpsichord, both the good and the bad[6]

The tone is comprised of two semitones, namely one minor and one major. The good minor third is composed of three semitones, namely two major semitones and one minor. The bad minor third is composed of two minor semitones and one major.[7] The good major third is composed of four semitones, two major and two minor. The bad major third is composed of four semitones, namely three major and one minor.[8] You may thus measure with a compass from rule to rule, or from semitone to semitone, on the table above. You can measure by the same means the difference between the tritone and the false fifth. The superfluous tone is composed of two major semitones.

6  The reader should note a slight peculiarity of Denis's *Table*: through some whim of the printer, the brackets that mark off the dimensions of the various intervals are indicated a bit oddly. For example, the bracket marking the 'good major third' intends to show that interval as C–E, though E does not appear to be included, and likewise for all the other brackets in the table.
7  As in the interval F–G♯ (actually an augmented second), which in quarter-comma meantone is 41.1 cents narrower than a 'good' minor third.
8  As in the interval F♯–B♭ (actually a diminished fourth), which in quarter-comma meantone is 41.1 cents wider than a 'good' major third.

# TREATISE ON THE TUNING
# OF THE HARPSICHORD

## With a comparison of its keyboard to vocal music

Man naturally delights in music. The more harmonious it is, the more it charms and gratifies the spirits it touches.

Our ancestors, having recognized that the human voice produced beautiful melodies, took pleasure in fashioning, for greater convenience, an instrument that could imitate the voice, or come as close to it as possible. All things considered, they could have taken up no instrument more appropriate than the harpsichord, though it was not yet known. But since they recognized the differences between tones by way of the voice, they began to create the keyboard, which is the most wonderful invention in the world and the means whereby music may be better comprehended. Music is based upon six monosyllables, namely *ut, re, mi, fa, sol, la,* and upon the interval defined by two of these syllables, *mi* and *fa,* which our ancestors placed just at the middle, as if to show that everything depends on these two.

They began to build a keyboard, that is, keys without *feintes*[9] or sharps. As proof of this, the *feintes* and sharps have no proper [solmization] syllables of their own, only those that they borrow from the [natural] keys. For example, C *sol, ut, fa* [C♮][10] has a *feinte* which is called the *feinte* of C *sol, ut, fa.* That of E *mi, la* [E♭] bears its own name, because on the [natural] key E *mi, la* there is no *fa* at all, which is the name of the *feinte.*[11] It is marked, like the one at

---

9 There is no satisfactory English equivalent for this term. See the Introduction, pp. 52–3.
10 The solmization syllables that follow each pitch name in Denis's treatise refer to the different positions a given note can occupy in the three hexachords of the Guidonian system. C *sol, ut, fa,* for example, can serve as *sol* in the 'soft' (with B♭) hexachord beginning on f, as *ut* in the 'natural' hexachord beginning on c, and *fa* in the 'hard' (with B♮) hexachord beginning on g. Notes like C that bear several solmization syllables also serve as pivot points, through which a musical line can shift from one hexachord into another by a process referred to as 'mutation'. Though they are perhaps a slight distraction to the modern eye, the solmization syllables are often crucial to the reader's comprehension of ideas discussed by Denis, and they have thus been retained throughout most of the translation.
11 E♭ had long since acquired its own solmization syllable, *fa.* According to the intervallic

61

B *fa*, b *mi*, and has all the same properties; both are designated thus: ♭. The others are marked ♯, one for F *ut*, *fa* and one for G *re*, *sol*, *ut*. The *feinte* at B *fa*, b *mi* [B♭] also carries its own name, because the [natural] key bears only the syllable *mi* in ascending and descending. In the gamut, only this scale degree has but one syllable [attached to it], namely B *fa*, which is the *feinte*, and b *mi*, which is the natural.[12]

Our ancestors, then, having made the keyboard without *feintes*, recognized that it would be good for only one genus, the diatonic, while in vocal music they could sing in three genera,[13] and they attempted to add the *feintes* of all the tones. And as they had made the keyboard without *feintes*, they added them everywhere.[14] In this

structure of Denis's scale (illustrated in the *Table* on p. 60), each of the *feintes* C♯, F♯, and G♯ is a minor semitone (76 cents in quarter-comma meantone) above its corresponding natural, and thus none of these can serve as *fa* in an ascending *mi–fa* major semitone (117.1 cents in quarter-comma meantone). Though E♮, as Denis remarks here, is not a *fa* in any mode or conventional transposition, E♭ functions as *fa* in the soft or 'ficta' hexachord b♭–c'–d'–e♭'–f'–g', which came into theoretical acceptance in the fourteenth and fifteenth centuries as the hexachord system was extended to provide modal species and finals in unaccustomed places. Gaffurius mentions the hexachord on b♭ (*Practica musice*, Milan, 1496, Book III, Ch. 13), as do a number of other theorists of the fifteenth century. E♭ was also required to satisfy the rule of *fa super la* in mutations involving the soft hexachord on F; an E♮ would have formed a tritone with the *fa* of the hexachord below (B♭–E).

12 All other diatonic scale degrees carry at least two solmization syllables; there can be no mutation into other hexachords from the notes B *fa* [B♭] or b *mi* [B♮]. This paragraph is the first of several in Denis's *Traité* that appear to have been adapted from the published writings of Marin Mersenne. See the first paragraph of *Observation IX* in Mersenne's *Nouvelles observations physiques et mathematiques* (Paris, ca. 1638, p. 22). Denis seems to have relied heavily on *Observation IX* in its entirety, though it is entirely possible that the ideas involved were originally expounded to Mersenne by none other than Jean Denis (see the Introduction, pp. 10–11). For a comparison of this and other parallel passages from Mersenne and Denis in the original versions, see Appendix A.

13 There was lively interest on the part of sixteenth- and seventeenth-century musicians and theorists in a revival of scale systems, or *genera*, based on the intervals of the diatonic, chromatic, and enharmonic tetrachords of Greek music.

14 Denis's attempt to summarize the history of keyboard design in a few sentences is inadequate at best. His mention of the attempt to add *feintes* 'everywhere' is presumably a reference to various attempts made in the fifteenth, sixteenth, and seventeenth centuries to construct keyboards with more than twelve notes per octave. Such arrangements generally fell into two categories: simpler schemes with divided accidentals to allow for additional pure thirds in quarter-comma meantone temperament, and more complicated arrangements that attempted to provide for justness of intonation and/or representation of the intervals of all three genera, through division of the octave into various numbers of equal or unequal microtones. In the *Harmonie universelle*, Mersenne discusses schemes for keyboards of 17, 19, 25, 27, and 32 notes per octave, and illustrates prototypes for all of these save the 25-division. See Mersenne, *Harmonie universelle*, vol. III, pp. 349–58. As an instrument maker, Denis would probably have been familiar with such experiments.

they were indeed frustrated and they recognized a confusion in the arrangement, for they were unable to place the *feintes* found between the *mi* and the *fa*, and they resolved to eliminate them entirely, as they were useless.[15]

It is an admirable and praiseworthy thing for them to have given each key its *feinte*, in such a way that none can be added or taken away; and as there were more naturals than *feintes*, to have given each natural its own, in an arrangement so splendid that no improvement is possible. Namely, for C *sol, ut, fa*, its *feinte*; for D *la, re, sol*, none at all, although there are three separate syllables for the single tone; for E *mi, la*, as it is set forth above; for F *ut, fa*, a *feinte*; for G *re, sol, ut*, a *feinte*; for A *mi, la, re*, none at all; for B *fa*, b *mi*, as it is explained above. The difference between flats and sharps is that flats descend from their naturals and sharps ascend.[16] When they saw that the naturals and the *feintes* were quite well arranged according to their sequence, they sought to devise a tuning, which is the subject of this treatise.

A man has come to this city of Paris who is very learned in mathematics, who believes that he has discovered the great secret of an arithmetical tuning, which he has hit upon through numbers.[17]

15 The *feintes* 'between the *mi* and the *fa*' (notes placed within the interval of a major semitone) were a feature of various theoretical systems for division of the octave. Salinas, for example, illustrates a 25-division that includes intervals of the diatonic, chromatic, and enharmonic genera. It calls for the E–F *semitonium diatonicum* (*mi–fa* major semitone, or 117.1 cents) to be divided into a *diesis chromatica* (minor semitone, or 76 cents) and a *diesis enharmonica* (41.1 cents). See Salinas, *De musica libri septem* (Salamanca, 1577), pp. 120–7. Mersenne discusses this division and reprints Salinas's intricate diagrammatic representation (*Harmonie universelle*, vol. II, *Livre troisiesme des genres*, pp. 163–5). In quarter-comma meantone, *feintes* between *mi* and *fa* were desirable in two places: between D and E♭, and G and A♭, resulting in an octave of fourteen notes. See the Introduction, pp. 36–43.

16 The scale that resulted was C, C♯, D, E♭, E, F, F♯, G, G♯, A, B♭, B, C. Each of the five *feintes* is a minor semitone away from its corresponding natural. Denis's assertion that each natural has its own *feinte* is inaccurate, and is quickly contradicted by his statement that neither D nor A has a corresponding *feinte*.

17 The system in question was twelve-note equal temperament. It is likely that the man to whom Denis refers was the inventor, mathematician, and author Jean Gallé of Liège, for Mersenne remarks that he knows of 'no one except Gallé' who has adapted equal temperament to the organ and the harpsichord (*Nouvelles observations*, p. 19). In a paragraph from the *Cogitata physico-mathematica* (p. 335), Mersenne characterizes equal temperament as the system that 'Gallé desired', but Denis 'could hardly tolerate'. Gallé's calculations for an equal-tempered octave of twelve notes are presented on page 21 of the *Nouvelles observations*, and are discussed in Appendix III to vol. V [1634] of the *Correspondance du P. Marin Mersenne*. In connection with equal temperament, Mersenne also mentions the geometer Jean Beaugrand, the astronomer Ismaël Boulliau,

He has presented it as good, and as superior to the harmonic tuning.[18] I shall demonstrate the opposite of this, showing that his tuning is worthless and that it is an artless tuning that can be carried out by anyone whose ear is good enough to tune a pure fifth.[19] This is the opposite of the harmonic tuning, which is so difficult that there are many accomplished harpsichordists and organists who would not venture to attempt the tuning of a harpsichord. There are some who do it well, but they are few indeed. The tuning of the harpsichord is the same as that of the organ. There is no difference, and the practitioners of each agree on this point. When I speak of one, I speak of the other as well.

Thus I declare that the harpsichord is the most perfect instrument of all instruments, for since it has many strings, each of which produces its own pitch, one can sound all the notes of music, pitch by pitch. The harpsichord with its keyboard can realize everything in written music, that which other instruments cannot accomplish unless there are several people and several instruments. A single

Gilles de Roberval (geometer and Professor of Mathematics at the Royal College), and an anonymous gentleman 'whose modesty is so great and so extraordinary that he does not wish to be named' (*Harmonie universelle*, vol. III, pp. 37–8, 384–7, and 408 respectively). For more on the calculations of Beaugrand and Boulliau, see Appendix I to vol. IV of the *Correspondance du P. Marin Mersenne*. A manuscript treatise on music by Boulliau is in the Library of the Observatoire de Paris (catalog number A, B, 5, 11). A manuscript treatise by de Roberval, the *Elementa musicae* (1651) is held in the Bibliothèque Nationale, Paris (MS fonds fr. 9119, fols. 374–470ᵛ).

18 This phrase, which later recurs in the text, is a reference to the meantone temperament advocated by Denis.

19 The reader should be warned that Denis introduces some confusion in his discussion of various tuning systems. There is the meantone temperament he advocates, described as 'our' tuning, the 'harmonic' tuning, and the 'good and perfect' tuning. He also refers to the tuning of the 'ancestors', saying that they tuned all the fifths pure and that the major thirds were too wide and were 'harsh'; this is apparently a reference to Pythagorean tuning. The third system mentioned is twelve-note equal temperament, the 'arithmetical' tuning being advocated by the 'learned' man newly arrived in Paris.

Based on the reference to the pure fifth in the footnoted sentence above, it appears that Denis has somehow confused Pythagorean and equal temperaments, and indeed they are superficially similar. Both have wide major thirds, and the slightly narrowed fifths of equal temperament (only two cents narrower than just fifths) might indeed have seemed 'pure'. Mersenne calls attention to that very point, remarking that the fifths of equal temperament are ' . . . so little diminished that it is almost impossible to distinguish them from just fifths' (*Nouvelles observations*, p. 19). Nevertheless, the tuning demonstration Denis later describes (p. 68) was clearly not a demonstration of Pythagorean tuning, a tuning which would by no means have 'agreed' with the conventional seventeenth-century tunings of lutes and viols, nor been 'good for transposing from semitone to semitone'. In point of fact, Denis's confusion echoes a statement in the passage from Mersenne from which he, Denis, was borrowing. See the second pair of passages in Appendix A.

organist can play music in four, five, six, seven, eight, nine, and ten parts, since he can employ ten fingers and two feet.[20] There is certainly no music in more than four or five parts that does not make some use of rests or unisons.

Let us speak of our tunings and their differences. Having perfected the keyboard, just as it is today, our ancestors wished to tune the harpsichord. They naively tuned all the fifths pure, which is the tuning that this man presents to us, as I indicated above.[21] When they proceeded to play, they found that this tuning was far from what they had expected. The major thirds were too wide, and were so harsh that the ear could not tolerate them. They found that there were no major or minor semitones whatsoever, but rather that there was a mean semitone, neither major nor minor, which was narrower than the major and wider than the minor. They found the cadences worthless, and since they were unable to endure this harshness that so violently offended the sense of hearing (which gives the greatest pleasure to our souls), they decided to temper this tuning so that the ear would be as pleased by instrumental music as by vocal music. Since they wished to narrow[22] the major thirds, it proved to be necessary to narrow all the fifths, and to temper them in a way that the ear could tolerate. I should mention that they did not make use of the theory of music, and that they did not have a

20 Only one organ composition in ten parts has survived, a setting by the German organist and theorist Arnolt Schlick (ca. 1460–after 1521) of the antiphon *Ascendo ad patrem meum* (MS Trent: Archivio di Stato, tedesca 105). A sentence in Schlick's dedicatory epistle was perhaps intended for those who might have assumed the piece to be 'eye' music only: 'And I have set the plainsong Ascendo ad patrem for ten voices, which can be played on the organ with four voices in the pedal and six in the manual, as I can demonstrate for eyes and ears.'

21 Denis seems to have confused Pythagorean tuning and equal temperament. See n. 19.

22 *baiser.* Much confusion arises in historical (and contemporary) writings on tuning and temperament when intervals are specified as being 'raised' or 'lowered', or are identified as being 'sharp' or 'flat'. Such terms can only apply to discrete pitches; an interval, being composed of two pitches, cannot be sharp or flat, only wide, narrow, or just. Nor can an interval be 'raised' or 'lowered'; these terms are properly applied only to the constituent pitches. Both Mersenne and Denis are guilty of these usages. In the *Harmonie universelle* (vol. III, p. 109), ambiguity results when Mersenne specifies that a particular meantone fifth is to be *augmentée*. Based on the evidence of later writings, he appears to have meant that its lower note (which is being tuned to the upper) should be raised in order to narrow the interval, but the passage can also be taken to mean that the lower note should be lowered to make the fifth wider. This particular confusion may well have influenced later French writings on keyboard temperament. See Lindley, 'Temperaments', *The New Grove* vol. xviii, p. 664, and 'Mersenne on Keyboard Tuning', *Journal of Music Theory* xxiv (1980), pp. 175–9.

monochord to determine the proportions. That I do not deny.[23] I do not wish to speak of theory at all, but only of practice and custom. When we tune the harpsichord to perfection (I say perfection because in this tuning nothing can be added or taken away without spoiling everything), we narrow all the fifths by a bit [*un poinct*][24] in such a way that the fifth still seems good, even though it is not pure. And over the sum of fifths, which are twelve in all, the others are nothing but duplicates.[25] They are all narrowed a bit, making it [the diminishment] as small as you would like. There must be twelve pitches, which is the difference from the first to the last fifth, and all the fifths must be tempered equally, all in like manner.[26]

The first interval is from the *feinte* of E *mi, la* [Eb] to its fifth B *fa* [Bb], which must be tuned flat, and from B *fa* to F *ut, fa*, which must also be tuned flat, and so on with the others, as practice teaches us. The last note is the *feinte* of G *re, sol, ut* [G#], which is the end of the tuning. All the octaves must be made pure, the octave being the most perfect interval of all.

Of these two tunings,[27] the better is the one that is closer to vocal music, namely our familiar harmonic tuning. It has all the major and minor tones and semitones, and cadences, in the same places and positions as they are when employed by the masters of music in

23 This paragraph appears to have been derived from Mersenne (*Nouvelles observations*, p. 22, *Observation IX*, para. 2). The reference to the monochord is a bit of snobbery or ignorance on Denis's part, as monochords had been in wide use since medieval times.

24 In the *Cogitata physico-mathematica*, Mersenne offers a tantalizing hint that this term may have referred to a specific amount of diminishment, namely one-quarter of the syntonic comma. See the Introduction, p. 30.

25 Only eleven fifths are actually tempered. The remaining interval G#–Eb, a diminished sixth rather than a fifth, is the musically unusable 'flaw [*deffaut*] of the tuning'. Interestingly, Mersenne makes a similar misstatement in the *Nouvelles observations*, in a passage Denis may well have been consulting as he wrote his own treatise. On p. 22, during a description of what is clearly strict quarter-comma meantone, Mersenne states that 'twelve fifths' are 'slightly narrowed'. Then, however, he identifies the last 'fifth' to be the interval G#–Eb, the wide diminished sixth which he, like Denis, terms the '*defaut de l'accord*'. See the second pair of passages in Appendix A. The G#–Eb interval is referred to as the 'wolf' by French and German musicians and theorists of the seventeenth century; in quarter-comma meantone, the 'wolf' fifth is 35.6 cents wider than a pure fifth and 41.1 cents wider than the quarter-comma meantone fifth.

26 This is the sentence that led Murray Barbour to claim Denis as a proponent of equal temperament (*Tuning and Temperament*, p. 47). In this context, however, 'all' clearly refers to the eleven fifths of meantone, not the twelve of equal temperament; in the next paragraph, Denis unequivocally defines an intonation system that extends only from Eb to G#, the pitch that is 'the end of the tuning'.

27 The presumably Pythagorean tuning of the 'ancestors' and the meantone temperament endorsed by Denis.

their compositions.[28] There is but one major tone and one superfluous tone. The major tone is made up of a major semitone and a minor semitone. The superfluous tone is made up of two major semitones, and musicians never make use of it at all. It is found in two places [on the keyboard], at the keys that have no *feintes* at all, namely D *la, re, sol* and A *mi, la, re*, which have a major semitone on either side.[29] All the other [natural] keys have a *feinte* of a minor semitone, which is the semitone that serves only for the chromatic [genus]. As for the enharmonic, it is not employed at all, either for singing or for the playing of instruments.[30]

The theorists distinguish three kinds of tones, namely the major tone, the minor tone, and the superfluous tone, as well as three kinds of semitones: the major semitone, the minor semitone, and the mean semitone. The minor tone and the mean semitone are not used at all. The minor tone is composed of a mean semitone and a minor semitone, and is smaller than the major tone. But in the practice of music, and in our harmonic tuning, neither the minor tone nor the mean semitone is found. The difference between the two tunings is that in the tuning that is proposed to us [equal tempera-

28 Denis has paraphrased Mersenne, who says that players 'observe two semitones in their keyboards, major and minor, in the same places where composers place them in their works for the voice' (*Nouvelles observations*, p. 23). Such remarks suggest that composers of the time were thinking in terms of the specific intervals of a common-practice temperament; indeed, the great majority of seventeenth-century keyboard works, even some of the most adventurously chromatic ones, do stay within the limitations of 12-note quarter-comma meantone temperament, as do the compositions of a sizeable polyphonic vocal repertoire. See Easley Blackwood, *The Structure of Recognizable Diatonic Tunings* (Princeton: Princeton University Press, 1985), pp. 179–87. Sample octaves displaying major and minor semitones placed identically to those of Denis are presented by Nivers (*Traité de la composition*, Paris, 1667, Part I, Ch. V) and D'Anglebert ('Principes de l'accompagnement' in *Pièces de clavessin*, Paris, 1689, p. 123).

29 Denis's superfluous tones, then, are the intervals C♯–E♭ and G♯–B♭ (diminished thirds in modern terminology). On this particular point, Denis's borrowing from the *Nouvelles observations* of Mersenne is direct and almost word-for-word. See the third pair of passages in Appendix A.

30 Apparently this was not always the case, for according to Galilei, Nicola Vicentino '. . . played a keyboard instrument that, in addition to the two ordinary manuals for the diatonic and chromatic, had another one to play the enharmonic. This Don Nicola moreover had a number of pupils who, particularly while he played the enharmonic, sang that genre of music composed by him. He let this music be heard in all the principal cities of Italy and I personally heard it at various times and places on a number of occasions. A sign of whether this music pleased or not is the fact that neither others nor his pupils put it into practice after his death' (Vincenzo Galilei, 'Discorso intorno all'uso dell'enharmonio' [Ms. ca. 1585], cited and translated by Claude Palisca, 'The Beginnings of Baroque Music; Its Roots in Sixteenth Century Theory and Polemics', unpublished dissertation, Harvard University, 1953, pp. 341–2).

ment], there is neither a major nor a minor semitone, but rather a mean semitone and a major tone similar to ours.[31] To make the mean semitone, the major semitone is narrowed. In so doing the minor semitone is widened, and in the process the semitones become equal.

At a gathering of very worthy persons I heard this tuning, which I found quite wretched and very harsh to the ear. When I told them my opinion, and that no one could find this satisfactory, they replied that I was not accustomed to it. I told them that if someone served them a banquet of tainted, bad-tasting meats and gave them vinegar to drink, they would have a right to complain. And if it were suggested to them that they were not accustomed to it, that would not be an adequate justification and would not be acceptable.

I wished to know what this tuning was good for. The man who had tuned told me that it was useful for playing the harpsichord, and for transposing from semitone to semitone, and that all chords were satisfactory throughout the compass, and that it agreed better than our tuning with the lute and the viol.[32] I told him that he was quite unjustified in wishing to spoil our good and perfect tuning in order to accommodate it to imperfect instruments, and that he should instead seek to perfect the lute and the viol, and find a way of making the semitones major and minor as we have them on the harpsichord. This is impossible to do with the tied frets[33] by which lutes are played, because they would have to be staggered [*faites en pieds de mousches*]. This can be accomplished with ivory frets,

31 The major tone of equal temperament is equivalent to 200 cents, while that of quarter-comma meantone is approximately 193.2 cents.
32 It appears that equal temperament, or a close approximation to it, was employed for the fretting of lutes and viols in France at this time. See Lindley, *Lutes, Viols and Temperaments*, pp. 78–80. A number of theorists of the sixteenth and seventeenth centuries, including Vicentino, Bottrigari, Doni, and Mersenne, remarked on the problems that resulted from attempts to combine keyboard instruments tuned in meantone with lutes and viols. See Lindley, pp. 43–50, and Mersenne, *Nouvelles observations*, p. 23.
33 *touches*. According to the *Dictionnaire mathématique* of Jacques Ozanam (Paris, 1691, p. 671), 'The small lengths of string that wrap around the necks of some stringed instruments are called *touches*, for one touches them with the fingers . . . '.

which can be located by the compass and according to the proportion of the monochord. In this fashion will the lute and the viol be brought into agreement with the harpsichord, in the musical and harmonic tuning.[34] But I do not think a sensible man would accept discord in place of a good tuning.

Some have considered it proper to say '*feintes*', while others prefer 'sharps', but the keys have both names. Understand that from the side of the major semitone it should be called a 'sharp' [*diese*], and from the side of the minor semitone it should be called a '*feinte*'[35] because it is nothing more than a feigned *fa*. And from the [natural] key to its own *feinte* there is only a minor semitone, some ascending and the others descending.

That is all that can be said about the tuning of the most beautiful and most perfect instrument in the world, given that it is impossible to compose music that it cannot express and perform all by itself, for there are harpsichords with two keyboards for passing all the

34 Denis has once again paraphrased Mersenne, who remarks in this regard that ' . . . the practitioners find the equal tuning very harsh because of the excessive size of the major thirds and the diminution of the [major] semitones. These detract from the stability and goodness of the cadences, which are also worthless on minor semitones. They believe that it is better to adjust the frets of the lute and the viol according to the monochord, so that they are perfectly in tune with the harpsichord, than to corrupt and destroy their tuning, whose harmony they find sweeter. They believe it would not be so difficult to place the said frets successfully on the neck of the lute (whether with frets of ivory or through the use of springs hidden inside or under the neck) . . . ' (*Nouvelles observations*, p. 23). Both authors are disappointingly vague regarding the precise method by which these auxiliary frets are to be placed and used, though Mersenne does suggest that lutes could employ ' . . . enharmonic frets, that could be played by pushing little springs with the thumb of the left hand, as I could demonstrate for those who wish to do so . . . ' (*Harmonie universelle*, vol. III, *Livre septiesme*, p. 60). This was evidently more than mere speculation, for Mersenne notes elsewhere that Jean Le Maire had actually modified the neck of a lute to obtain a 24-division of the octave, using 'little springs behind the neck that are touched by the thumb' (*Harmonie universelle*, vol. II, *Livre sixiesme de la Rythmique*, p. 439). More revealing than any of this, perhaps, is Mersenne's statement that although equal temperament on the lute was convenient, the practitioners also adjusted the frets up or down 'according to the judgment of their ears' (*Harmonie universelle*, vol. III, p. 61).
35 This is a muddled explanation, perhaps based on a careless reading of Mersenne, who states the case correctly: 'One may call the *feintes* that make the minor semitone *dieses*, in order to distinguish them from those that make the major [semitone]' (*Nouvelles observations*, p. 23).

unisons,[36] a thing that the lute cannot do. Organs have four keyboards,[37] for playing all sorts of music.

Others have said that to tune the harpsichord in this scheme that is proposed to us, *ut, re, mi, fa, sol, la* must be tuned from key to key, as the voice directs us.[38] I say that this is quite incorrect, because this is to tune in the manner of the flageolet, which is tuned without trial intervals [*preuves*]. But since the harpsichord has a keyboard and the potential for trial intervals, we wrong the instrument if we do not take advantage of its properties. The flageolet, as I said, has not one sound that can be tested against another, nor does the unaccompanied voice.

When I have found myself in gatherings, people have not been inclined to listen to me, for I am considered a simple artisan. However, since I am an organist as well as an artisan, and since I encounter persons who discuss these matters and do not know what they are talking about, I have written this modest volume. I trust that the reader will receive it as readily as his servant, with all good intentions, offers it.

36 *pour passer tout les unissons.* This is apparently a reference to the crossing of voices that can be accomplished only on a harpsichord with two independent manuals (an instrument with two keyboards, two sets of 8 foot strings, and a manual coupler rather than dogleg jacks, so that each unison 8 foot stop can be played independently). The *pièces croisées* of Louis Couperin (ca. 1650) are the first surviving harpsichord pieces that require such a disposition. According to extant contracts, manual couplers began to appear in French organs in the first half of the sixteenth century, though the mechanics of such arrangements are not specified. See Norbert Dufourcq, *Le livre de l'orgue français, Tome III: La facture* (Paris, 1975), p. 47. In the Preface to his *Hymnes de l'Eglise* (1623), Jehan Titelouze notes that '. . . for some years now, [French organs] have been made with two separate manuals for the hands and a pedal keyboard . . . with which it is possible to express [*exprimer*] the unison, the crossing of parts, and all sorts of musical figures . . . '. Despite this statement, none of the pieces in the *Hymnes de l'Eglise* actually calls for crossing of the hands on different manuals.

37 At the time Denis was writing (1643 in this section), the 'four keyboards' would most likely have included *Grand-Orgue, Positif, Écho* or *Récit,* and *Pédale.* The third manual keyboard, the *Écho* or *Récit,* began to appear in French organs after 1610. Unlike the *Brustwerk* manuals of contemporary Dutch and North German instruments, the third manual of the French organ did not control a complete division at first, but instead played only a single *jeu,* the *dessus de cornet,* borrowed from the great. The keyboard was usually limited to 25 notes (c′–c′′′), and was coupled permanently to the great. See Peter Williams, *The European Organ* (London: Batsford, 1966), pp. 176–82, and Dufourcq, *Le livre de l'orgue français, Tome III,* pp. 112–14, 181.

38 Denis has probably picked up this puzzling notion of tuning procedure from the *Nouvelles observations,* for Mersenne several times mentions 'beginning by *ut, re, mi,* &c.' when tuning equal temperament (*Nouvelles observations,* pp. 18, 20, 23). Neither author goes any further to clarify how such a method would have worked.

# Procedure for tuning the harpsichord properly [39]

One must begin with f, and then tune its octave pure. After that tune c', a fifth from f, and make it completely pure. Then lower it just enough that it still seems good and the ear can tolerate it. From c', tune its lower octave pure. Then tune its fifth g in the same way, narrowing it to the same degree as the first. Then tune its upper octave pure, which is g'. Tune d', and then tune this fifth in the same way, narrowing it like the others. Then pause at this point and perform the trial, which is done in this way. Tune b♭, next to c', to the fifth f', next to g', and keep the b♭ a bit high, so that this fifth is tempered [*temperée*] and is the same as the others. Then play the d' that you have tuned, which makes the major third against b♭ and the minor third against f'. When this chord is found to be good, everything which has been tuned is good, because the tuning is proven only by the thirds. When they are found to be good throughout, the tuning is correct.

Continue then, and follow the order used at the beginning. Go by octaves and fifths to the last note, and do not tune any fifth after the first trial mentioned above if the third within it does not prove to be good, as you may observe in the example that follows.

The first note from which all the fifths are narrowed is the *feinte* of e [e♭] and the last is the *feinte* of g' [g'♯].[40] Thus will all the notes in the middle of the keyboard be in tune, both naturals and *feintes*. Continue then to the bass and the treble by octaves, from natural to natural and from *feinte* to *feinte*, always testing with thirds and fifths.[41]

---

39 For the sake of clarity in this chapter, the solmization syllables that accompany note names in the original treatise have been dropped. Here c' stands for Middle C, c for the note an octave lower, c″ for the note an octave higher.
40 This sentence refers not to the order of the tuning procedure, but rather to the tonal dimensions of Denis's meantone system.
41 Modern-day tuners would do well to heed this piece of advice. When tuning quarter-comma meantone, fifths are particularly useful for checking the accuracy of newly tuned notes in the bass and treble.

# How the Harpsichord and the Prestant
## of the Organ should be tuned

Then continue by octaves, as in the account above.

# The translation

*Prelude* for determining whether the tuning is good throughout

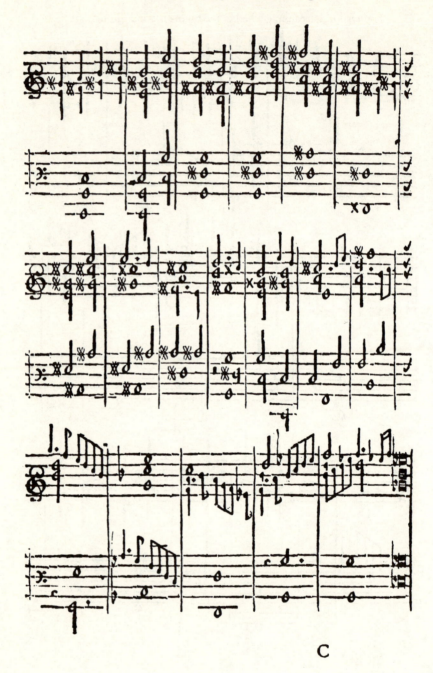

C

74

# Advice to choirmasters and organists

Having spoken of the tuning of the harpsichord and the organ and having demonstrated how it is perfect in its intervals, all of them uniform in their nature,[42] it must be understood that organists must never transpose either the *tons* of the church or the modes of music except to the customary notes or keys.[43] Choirmasters must not and cannot force them to do otherwise (though organists should know how to transpose to any note, in order to show that they are able to do so). Because in transposing the first [*ton*] to E *mi, la,* it must be admitted that the final cadence is worthless, as it is made on a minor semitone.[44] The major third of that cadence is also worthless, being larger than a major third. The major third is made up of two whole and equal tones, while the superfluous third is made up of a major tone and a superfluous tone.[45] It is consequently too wide and is worthless, as is the cadential trill.

The organist must under no circumstances transpose to or play in that *ton*, nor in the second [*ton*] on F *ut, fa,* because the minor third, composed of a major tone and a minor semitone, is too narrow and is worthless, and because a superfluous tone must be employed, playing *re* [on] F *ut, fa; mi* on G *re, sol, ut; fa* as the *feinte* of G *re, sol, ut,* which is the worthless minor semitone; *sol* on B *fa,*

42 In the regular meantone temperament that Denis advocates, all intervals of a particular name are the same in size, regardless of where they occur in the scale and on the keyboard. See the Introduction, pp. 31–2.

43 In light of subsequent comments, Denis appears to be ruling out transpositions that would call for enharmonic notes outside the standard 12-note meantone octave.

44 The scale set out by Denis does not provide enharmonic equivalence and does not include the requisite D♯ leading tone. In quarter-comma meantone the existing E♭, a 'minor semitone' away from E, is too sharp by the amount of the lesser or enharmonic diesis (41.1 cents). Employed in the cadence in question, the E♭ would have resulted in a jarring discordance that would indeed have made the cadence 'worthless'.

45 Denis's 'superfluous third', in this case b–e♭', is in fact a diminished fourth, a pronounced dissonance in quarter-comma meantone temperament. This dissonant interval was nevertheless purposely employed in certain contexts by seventeenth-century keyboard composers (see the Introduction, pp. 32, 35–6).

which is the superfluous tone; and *la* [on] C *sol, ut, fa*.[46] But reflection will reveal that here is the way to make a fine musical madness. And because all the harmonic consonances are dissonant and discordant, it is senseless for organists to play them. The major third, minor third, major sixth, minor sixth, and the minor semitone of *mi, fa*[47] are all discords that offend the ear.

Organists must not under any circumstances play in these [transposed] *tons*, and choirmasters should use discretion, taking care to come to agreement with the organist regarding proper and harmonious pitches and intervals.[48] They should not, for the sake of a simple *faux-bourdon*, preclude all the inventions of the organist's skill – the freedom of the hands, the execution of fine passagework, the sudden attacks, *coulemens*[49] and ornaments[50] that lend grace to playing – and they should not spoil the tuning of the organ, which is so perfect. Such a requirement is not reasonable. The canons of chapters where there is music should, for their satisfaction, take care that the organist is able to play with freedom, so that the service

46 In the second *ton* transposed to F, an A♭ would have been necessary, and the intervals and chords involving the existing G♯ were unacceptable. The interval F–G♯ is not a minor third, but rather an augmented second, 41.1 cents narrower than the minor third in quarter-comma meantone. On p. 155 of the *Syntagma Musicum*, vol. II, Michael Praetorius addresses the same problem and suggests, in lieu of a split key for G♯/A♭, that G♯ be raised to a compromise pitch between the two notes. To modern ears, the resulting adjustment is tolerable but by no means fully satisfactory. For additional comments by Praetorius on the problems caused by the absence of D♯ and A♭ in organs and harpsichords, see the *Syntagma Musicum*, vol. III, p. 81.

47 As in the above example, where the minor semitone G–G♯ could not serve as a *mi–fa* major semitone.

48 One hundred years earlier, Pietro Aaron had offered similar cautions to *maestri di capelli*, and warned that they must consider the limitations of the organ (*Lucidario in musica*, pp. 37–8). At that time, auxiliary keys and pipes for D♯ and A♭ were apparently still lacking in many Italian organs. See the Introduction, p. 37.

49 According to Nivers, this term refers to an effect created by connecting notes more closely than with the then-standard keyboard articulation (though not necessarily playing them in a modern 'over-legato' fashion, since the composer specifies that the notes must still be 'distinguished'). For a discussion of the technique, with examples, see Nivers's Introduction to his first *Livre d'orgue* (Paris, 1665). In his discussion, Nivers recommends that organists should model their ornaments and diminutions after vocal practice, ' . . . for in these instances the organ should imitate the voice'.

50 *accents*. By the beginning of the eighteenth century the term *accent* had acquired a specific meaning in French theoretical writings, and usually referred to a single-note grace also known variously as the *aspiration* or *plainte* (see M. de St Lambert, *Les principes du clavecin* [Paris, 1702], pp. 56–7). In the first half of the seventeenth century, however, *accent* seems to have been employed as a generic term for 'ornament'. For example, in his Introduction to the *Hymnes de l'Eglise*, Titelouze remarks that *accents* 'enliven' the parts, but that ' . . . the difficulty of setting type for all the notes that would be required has compelled me to leave them to the judgment of the player . . . '.

of God in the holy church may be performed with harmonious melody.

This lesson is not original with me. I learned it from my master, who was the most excellent man of his time in organ playing and also in the composition of vocal music. He was organist of the Sainte-Chapelle in Paris,[51] and his name was Florent le Bienvenu.[52] Once when I was with him at the organ, I put this question to him: 'Sir, why do you play the antiphon of the Magnificat in one *ton* and the Magnificat in another?' He told me that he performed the plain-chant so as to suit the singers.[53] As for the Magnificat, he said, 'The choirmaster of this church tried to make me accommodate my playing to his convenience. I refused to do so, and I told him, "You wish to sing at your convenience, and I wish to play at mine".' He also told me, 'It will happen that people from Italy, from England, from Spain, and who knows where else, will come to listen to me, and they will think that I have performed nothing worthwhile, even if I have played like an angel, because in those *tons* the organ sounds out of tune'.[54] Therefore organists should never play thus, because he who was so expert refused to do so.

End of the first book.[55]

---

51 A contemporary drawing of the Sainte-Chapelle organ in the late sixteenth century (J. Cellier, Bibliothèque Nationale Ms. fr. 9152, fol. 90) is reproduced as Plate XXVII in Norbert Dufourcq, *Le livre de l'orgue français*, Tome II: *Le buffet*.

52 Florent Bienvenu (born Florent Helbic, Rouen 1568–Paris 1623), who served as canon at the Cathedral of Laon before becoming organist of the Sainte-Chapelle, Paris, in 1597. During his early years in Rouen, it is likely that Bienvenu was in contact with Titelouze, and may have been his pupil. For more on Bienvenu, see Pierre Hardouin, 'Notes biographiques sur quelques organistes parisiens des XVII^e et XVIII^e siècles: Florent Bienvenu', *L'Orgue* lxxxii (January–March 1957), pp. 1–7. Various archival references to Bienvenu and his tenure at the Sainte-Chapelle are collected in Michel Brenet, *Les musiciens de la Sainte-Chapelle du Palais* (Paris, 1910), pp. 147–66 *passim*.

53 Bienvenu apparently chose to play his interpolated Magnificat versets at pitch levels that did not require notes (D♯ and A♭) apparently unavailable on his instrument. Denis later amplifies this point in his discussion of the third *ton*, p. 85.

54 Surviving employment contracts for Parisian organists reflect that the organist himself was often held responsible for keeping the instrument in tune. If this was the case for Bienvenu, he would have been well aware that sour harmonies would suggest not only a lack of playing skill on his part, but incompetence in tuning as well.

55 The 1643 edition of the *Traité de l'accord de l'espinette* ended at this point. All subsequent material appeared in the 1650 edition only.

# On the quantity and diversity of sounds

Wishing to give pleasure to all those who love music, I have considered and thoroughly investigated everything related to all sounds that make harmony and are able to create concord and consonance to be judged by the sensibility of the ear. I have been able to find nothing save what has already been created, and having thought it over carefully, [I believe that] it is impossible to create anything new which is not derived from the four universal sounds. They are: first, the human voice; second, the sound of the organ, which comes from air and wind; third, the sound of strings, whether of steel, gold, silver, brass, or gut; and fourth, the sound of the hammer, which is the sound of bells and of the drum. Beyond these four it is impossible to discover any others.

It might be objected that birds possess quite pleasing and delightful voices, and even that some speak and sing songs quite well, which is true. But these songs must not be elevated to the category of music, given that birds do not and cannot create either harmony or consonance. To create harmony, there must be two or three voices that produce various intervals and sound in proper tune according to the judgment of the ear. To attempt to attribute this to birds would be crediting them with the use of reason.

A man tried to teach two parrots to sing. He taught the treble of a song to one, and the bass to the other. After he took great pains to make them sing accurately, the one that sang the treble sang quite well, and the one that sang the bass also sang very well. It was an amusing curiosity to observe this man with his two parrots; I will leave you to judge which of the three was the wisest. For when the man began to sing the treble, in order to make his treble parrot begin singing, the bird would have no part of it. When the man saw that was a lost cause, he set about singing the bass in order to start the parrot that knew it. The bird was moved to sing, but his companion listened to him and uttered not a sound. The man started to sing the treble, harmonizing with his bass parrot, in order to make the other one sing. But the parrot singing the bass, hearing the man sing, began to listen. And after taking all this trouble, the man had no idea of how to make them sing together. It would have been necessary to credit them with the use of reason, as I mentioned above.

# Two remarkable tales honoring music

### THE FIRST, CONCERNING A WHITE PEACOCK

This was told to me by a man who honored me with his friendship, and whom I held in great esteem. He was of my profession, a builder of musical instruments. He told me that a gentleman near Paris had once sent a footman to him, to ask that a Bolognese lute[56] he had seen at the shop be sent to his home, and to ask that the builder come to make merry, along with a master lutenist whom he named but whose name I have forgotten. The builder gave the lute to the footman, and promised to visit and to bring this lutenist along with him.

Leaving Paris after noon on a Saturday, they arrived at the said gentleman's estate and were very well received. They passed the remainder of the day, and the next morning the lutenist rose earlier than the others. As he went into the garden, he heard a Mass being sung in the Church, and he attended it. Upon his return he took up his lute to entertain himself, as he was alone. He strolled about, thinking only of the harmony of the lute. As soon as he entered the garden, he noticed a white peacock at his side, which turned its head gracefully and regarded him attentively. Noting this, he decided to see whether the bird took pleasure in harmony. He intentionally moved about, from the garden to the vineyard, from the vineyard to the orchard, now here, now there, through many and diverse places, and returned to the manor. The peacock, ever attentive, continued to follow him throughout. The lutenist, having been conscientious and having attended the first Mass, had this pleasant experience while the others were attending the second Mass. When they returned from the church they sat down to dinner, which is customary as you know. Over dessert, he who had enjoyed the favor of the

---

56 Besides dealing in their own wares, Parisian luthiers of the seventeenth century also imported and sold Italian instruments, which were much in demand. See Catherine Massip, *La vie des musiciens de Paris au temps de Mazarin* (Paris: Éditions A. et J. Picard, 1976), p. 129.

peacock began to recount to the company the tale you have already heard. They began to laugh and told him that he, not knowing what to do, had concocted a tall tale that was clearly a fabrication. They made sport of him, laughing heartily.

After assuring them that what he had spoken was true, he took up his lute as they left the table and said to them, 'Let us go and see whether the peacock is of a mind to hear the sound of the lute.' They searched for the peacock in the courtyard, but it was nowhere to be found. Thinking to ridicule this lutenist, they said to him, 'Play! Play your lute! He will come!' As soon as he started to play, the peacock, which was on a wall, heard the sound of the lute and came in full flight to the player. It began to follow him in the same manner it had adopted in the morning, remaining always at his side.

The entire company was quite astonished to observe this bird so attentive to the harmony of the lute. They were delighted, and marveled at the way it followed the man everywhere with singular attention. But this is not what ought to be appreciated. It must be concluded that this peacock took pleasure not only in the sound of the lute, but in the consonances and the harmony as well, as you shall hear.

After this entertainment the company spent the rest of the day at other amusements. At dinner the following day, when the group was at the table, a page decided to have a bit of fun with the peacock. Taking up the lute, which he could not play at all, he scratched out a ditty in his own fashion. The peacock did not fail to come as usual, and for a while it followed the page. Remarkably, however, when it realized that the page was playing nothing worthwhile, and when it no longer heard any harmonies or consonance, it hurled itself upon the page with talons, beak, and wings, in such a way that it made him drop the lute and dash terror-stricken to the house!

Those who saw him so alarmed asked him what was wrong, and what he was afraid of. He told them what the peacock had done to him, and that the peacock had flung itself upon the lute to smash it. At that they rushed off to see whether it was true, and seeing that it was, they chased the peacock away to keep the poor lute from being broken to pieces, though it already had cracked sides and a shattered soundboard. All those in the company could not believe what they were seeing, so extraordinary and incredible was the affair. I have been assured that this is true, which is why I have related it to you here.[57]

### ANOTHER TALE, OF A MELANCHOLY LADY

One day, when I was at a house where I had been summoned to regulate a harpsichord, a worthy gentleman came and spoke to me, saying that the harpsichord was a fine instrument and that music was a marvelous thing. And then he recounted to me an experience he had had. He told me that he had a very virtuous and good-natured wife who had fallen into a long and grievous illness. She had finally recovered her health, but a great melancholy remained with her, one so peculiar that she took no pleasure in anything. She lay always in her bed with the curtains closed and wished to see no one. This greatly distressed her husband and all his servants, since before her sickness she had been quite merry.

When her husband complained to one of his friends, saying that this troubled him very much, the friend asked him whether he had consulted a good doctor regarding this matter. He told his friend that he had tried every means and all sorts of medicines in trying to restore his wife to her former health, and that he had given up hope of seeing her again in her previous disposition.

The gentleman replied that since all kinds of remedies had been attempted, he wished to propose a plan that would in his opinion succeed in curing his friend's wife. 'Speak', he said, 'to the Master who leads the King's ensemble of twenty-four violins. Tell him that you wish to offer the pleasure of their music to a person whom you wish to please, and that he should take time to ensure that their instruments are well tuned in advance, so that this music may come as a surprise to the person whom you wish to have hear it. It isn't necessary to explain the circumstances to the musicians, only to request clearly that they not sound their violins until they begin in earnest, and all together.'

This was so cleverly done that everything succeeded wonderfully well. A piece of tapestry had been hung quite close to the bed, and a time was chosen when the lady was not asleep. The violins all

---

57 The moral of the story, it would seem, is that peacocks ought to be brought along to concerts and recitals.

began together. The force of these instruments, which twenty-four men made to sound with all their strength and with great intensity, surprised the lady greatly, for it was the last thing she expected. This harmony made such an impact that it instantly banished her baleful melancholy. She recovered her former health and her merry disposition.

The gentleman related this story to me with much ardor and feeling, and after he told it to me in such a way I believed it to be the truth. Observe in these two tales how benevolent and wondrous is the power of harmony: a bird recognized lovely melodies, beautiful consonances, and harmony, as opposed to the dissonances, the twanging, and the discords of the page, and the lady was cured of the great melancholy which had confined her for so long. Thus is it amply demonstrated that music is a most excellent thing. Some men have told me they would hasten ten leagues[58] to hear a good performance. Others have said thirty leagues, and whenever there has been notable music-making, in which I take a great interest, I have always encountered them there, which convinces me that what they say is true.

58 Twenty-five miles.

# The eight *tons* of the church

I have not encountered an author who has written a treatise on the *tons* sung in the church (which the organist should know) who has been able to clear up the question of their ranges for those who wish to learn. That is why I have decided to write about them: how I have learned them, and how they are observed in the plainchant sung in churches; how organists should play them and end them for the convenience of the choir; and afterward, how fugues and subjects should be treated.

First of all, it should be known that those who composed the antiphons and the chants of psalmody employed only the diatonic [genus], which is one of the three genera of music, as you may read above. As a result, they used only the naturals of the keyboard and did not make use of the *feintes* or sharps, so as not to present so much difficulty to those who wished to learn to sing the plainchant. However, they did observe the B♭, and made it known that anything sung above *la* should be sung as *fa*, which is quite wrong if it is not marked. Anyone who sings music or plainchant is obliged to sing only what he sees written down.[59] To do otherwise would be to compose, not to sing, as I could prove through numerous examples.

The order of the *tons*, and their proper notes.

| | |
|---|---|
| The first *re, la*. | The fifth *fa, fa*. |
| The second *re, fa*. | The sixth *fa, la*. |
| The third *mi, fa*. | The seventh *ut, sol*. |
| The fourth *mi, la*. | The eighth *ut, fa*. |

One must know on which notes the psalms, the Magnificat, and the Benedictus must begin and end according to the *tons* of the antiphons.

---

59 Michael Praetorius, Pietro Aaron and other earlier theorists also favored the writing out of all accidentals. See Praetorius, *Syntagma Musicum*, vol. III, p. 31, and Pietro Aaron, *Toscanello de la Musica* (Venice, 1523), Book II, Chapter 20 and *Aggiunta* (supplement to the 1529 edition).

The first *ton* begins on D *la, re, sol*, its dominant is A *mi, la, re*, and its mediant is F *ut, fa*.

According to the Antiphoner, the second [*ton*] should also begin on D *la, re, sol*. But for the convenience of the choir, the organist should play it on G *re, sol, ut*, with the B♭. Its [distinguishing] notes are *re* on G *re, sol, ut* and the dominant *fa* on B *fa*, which is a fourth higher than its untransposed position.[60]

For the third, which is sung *mi, fa*, it must be understood that the *mi* that is the first note is on E *mi, la*, and its dominant is on C *sol, ut, fa*, the clef [Middle C], which is a minor sixth, contrary to the opinion of many, who believe it to be a semitone.[61] This is the case for the antiphon only. For the Magnificat and for the Benedictus it begins[62] on G *re, sol, ut*, its dominant is C *sol, ut, fa*, and it ends on A *mi, la, re*. But for the convenience of the singers it should be played on F *ut, fa* with the B♭, its dominant on B *fa*, and ended on G *re, sol, ut*.[63]

The fourth [*ton*] begins with *mi*, on E *mi, la*, and its dominant is A *mi, la, re*. This *ton* is called arithmetic, meaning that it has its fourth below, contrary to all the others, and has no perfect cadence.[64] It alone does not have one, and it ends on E *mi, la*.

The fifth [*ton*], which is *fa, fa*, begins on F *ut, fa*, its dominant is on C *sol, ut, fa*, the clef, and it ends on A *mi, la, re*. But for the convenience of the choir it is begun on C *sol, ut, fa*, its dominant is on G *re, sol, ut*, and it ends on C *sol, ut, fa*.

The sixth [*ton*] begins on F *ut, fa*, its dominant is on A *mi, la, re*, and it ends on F *ut, fa*, with the B♭.

---

60 A reciting tone of *fa* on f was evidently too low for the choir, a problem corrected by the transposition.

61 The dominant is indeed *fa*, but the *fa* of the hexachord beginning on g, into which it was necessary to move through mutation.

62 For the *choir*. See Thomas Connolly, 'Psalm' (II), *The New Grove*, vol. xv, p. 325.

63 The choir's sung antiphon began and ended on e. An organ interlude came next, followed by the beginning of the Magnificat or Benedictus by the choir on g. Denis recommends this transposition for the organist so that the choir can receive its beginning note from the last note played by the organist. Such a transposition, like some of the others later mentioned, does not preserve the intervallic structure of the original *ton* (the third *ton* on e begins with a major semitone). It is clear that in the *tons* as described by Denis and Nivers, placement of dominants and finals was the most significant consideration; the precise sequence of half and whole steps that came between was not as important.

64 On organs not equipped with a split key for D♯–E♭, the D♯ leading tone necessary for a perfect cadence was lacking.

The untransposed seventh [*ton*] begins on G *re, sol, ut*, its dominant is on D *la, re, sol*, and it extends up as far as F *ut, fa*, next to the clef of G *re, sol, ut*. [Chants in this *ton*] terminate and end on various notes in many different ways, but the organist should always end it on G *re, sol, ut*, with the Bb, and let the choristers sing it as written in their books.[65]

The eighth [*ton*] begins on G *re, sol, ut*, and its dominant is on C *sol, ut, fa*, and it ends on G *re, sol, ut*, with the Bb. But for the convenience of the choir it should be played on F *ut, fa*, with the Bb, and with the flat throughout.

It is indeed difficult to write of a science about which no one has yet written. All those who practice it lack certainty, and even in discussions with the learned there are differences of opinion. For example, I saw a fugue or subject given to three organists, as follows.

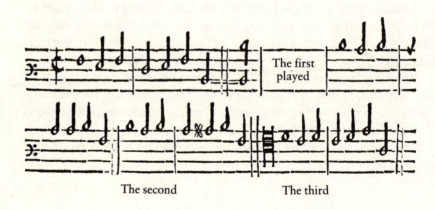

The first
played

The second                    The third

<hr />

65  In *ton* VII the choir's chants often began on notes other than the finalis. In such instances the organist could have been most helpful by ending on the choir's dominant, which remained consistent, rather than on the finalis. Since the choir would have transposed the *ton* to c, with g as dominant and one flat in the signature, the organist ended on g and allowed the choir to find its own pitch. The organist was compelled to play with a Bb in this case, as a B♮ would have conflicted with the Bb sung by the choir.

The translation

The third of these was judged to have done best, even though he departed from his octave. But it must be borne in mind that the note which exceeds the octave makes a cadence on the dominant. That is why he was very favorably judged, though had he been taking an examination he would have been failed.[66]

---

66 At this time musicians were still mindful of the precept that subject and answer should outline the mode, and that the answer should not exceed the ambitus of the mode (see Nivers, *Traité de la composition*, p. 50, and Charles Masson, *Nouveau traité des règles pour la composition de la musique* [Paris, 1697], pp. 105–6). The difficulty here arose with the attempt to compress the given subject into the fourth a–d' to form a tonal answer; some adjustment of the subject's intervals was clearly necessary. The third note in the final measure of the example is the note that 'exceeds the octave' – in this instance, e' in a fugue in the first *ton*. This e' does indeed provide for a 'cadence on the dominant', being a fifth above a. The third organist came closest to preserving the intervals of the subject, and this was perhaps the reason that he was 'very favorably judged'.

# Treatise on fugues,
# and how they should be realized [I]

Having explained above the order and ranges of the *tons* and having shown their beginning notes, their dominants, and their mediants, there follows a description of the category of fugues: how many kinds there are, and how the second part should be made to enter following the first.

Two things must be noted and observed diligently in all sorts of fugues: the second part that enters must have as many notes as the first, with the same stress and the same rhythm;[67] and secondly the *fa* must be played [in the answer] as many times, and in the same position, as in the subject.[68]

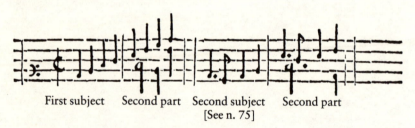

First subject    Second part    Second subject    Second part
[See n. 75]

Since you see that the *fa* in the first subject is the second note, the second part has its *fa* as the second note, and the second subject has its *fa* as the fourth note. There are those who will remark that I am saying nothing new, and that it could not be done otherwise. I will demonstrate the contrary, using the example of an organist who was summoned to play the organ of a parish church in the Office for

---

67 This rule is echoed by de La Voye-Mignot, who states that each of the voices in a fugue 'must have the same rhythm [*qualité*], that is to say the parts must follow each other with the same note values [*par mesme couleur de nottes*]' (*Traité de la musique* [Paris, 1656], p. 109). Neither Denis nor de La Voye-Mignot explicitly refers to the intervallic alterations necessary to form tonal answers.

68 This second rule is echoed by Charles Masson, who remarks that 'One must take care to ensure that the half step in the subject (if it has one) comes at the same note in the answer; that is to say, if the half step is at the third note of the subject, it should also be placed at the third note of the answer.' See Masson, *Nouveau traité des règles*, p. 109.

the Dedication of a Church. This organist should have been ready and prepared, but he made this mistake in one of the versets of the hymn.

Subject                    Second part

Observe through this example that those who consider themselves to be the most learned are those who commit the greatest errors. Instead of observing the harmonic in the fourth *ton*, they wish to observe the arithmetic, and instead of beginning the second part at the fifth, they seek to begin it at the fourth, as you see. If this organist had begun [the second part] on B♮ instead of beginning on A *mi, la, re*, he would have succeeded. That is why the number of notes must be carefully observed, and also the *fa* and the position in which it should be, as I have explained above. Do not play a *mi* instead of a *fa*.[69]

That will serve as a warning to those who attempt to create fugues, and next you will see how to proceed in constructing and carrying out fugues in all the *tons*. It must be pointed out that fugues can begin at the unison, at the fifth, or at the octave, at the player's discretion.

For the first *ton*, which we have said to be *re, la*:

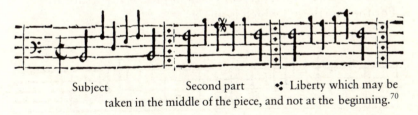

Subject                    Second part     ⁘ Liberty which may be
taken in the middle of the piece, and not at the beginning.[70]

69 Interestingly, Denis's later examples for fugues in the fourth *ton* (p. 90) both show answers beginning on a. The error he is attempting to point out here is not that the organist chose an improper starting note for his answer, but rather that he did not play *fa* in the same place in both subject and answer, a rule followed in Denis's own examples.
70 The 'liberty' referred to here is the playing of the note e' (the penultimate note of the third measure), a note that 'exceeds the octave' of the *ton*.

Another subject in the first *ton*     Second part

The second *ton* is the same as the first, except that it is transposed [up] a fourth, and should be played on G *re, sol, ut,* with the B♭. Two fugues follow in the second *ton,* which is *re, fa.*

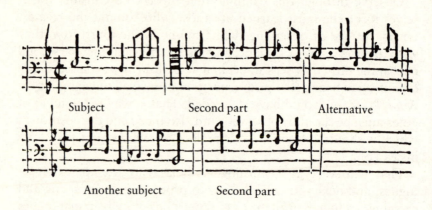

Subject          Second part          Alternative

Another subject          Second part

As to the third [*ton*], which is *mi, fa,* it should be played on G *re, sol, ut,* with the B♭, and is completely identical to the second *ton.* That is why I shall present no examples or fugues for it.

For the fourth *ton,* which is *mi, la:*

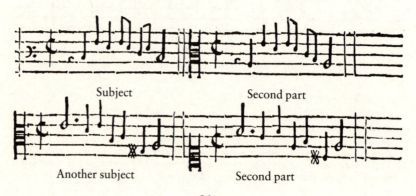

Subject          Second part

Another subject          Second part

For the fifth, which is *fa, fa*, it must be understood that it begins on F *ut, fa* and ends on A *mi, la, re*, according to the Antiphoner, but the organist should play it on C *sol, ut, fa*, and end it on C *sol, ut, fa* as well.

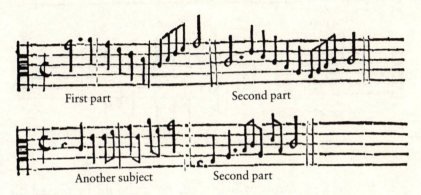

As to the sixth, which is *fa, la*, it is played on F *ut, fa*.

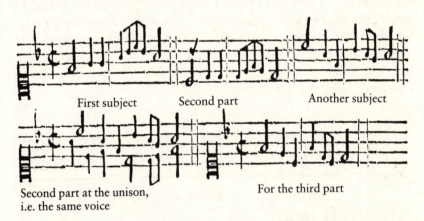

As regards the seventh, which is *ut, sol*, this is the most difficult to execute, and I have seen very skilled organists realize it with B♮. But it should be realized with B♭. Since the melody of the psalmody has the B♭, here is a fugue which has the range of the said *ton*.[71]

---

71 B♮ would have been correct if the seventh *ton* had been played on g. As we have seen earlier, however (n. 65), the choir would have transposed the plainsong down a fifth to c, bringing a flat to the signature. Denis's examples here reflect that transposition.

First part                     Second part

Another subject

❖ I have written this second part with the
counterpoint as an example, because it is very difficult to realize.

As for the eighth *ton*, which is *ut, fa*, it should be played on
F *ut, fa*, with the B♭, and with the flat throughout. It must be understood that this *ton* is arithmetic rather than harmonic. If it is treated
harmonically it will not be the eighth *ton*, it will be the sixth. To
clarify the difference, the sixth has C *sol, ut, fa*, as its dominant,[72]
which is the fifth above, and the eighth has its fifth below, as B *fa*,
and [in] all the fugues that begin with F *ut, fa*, the second part should
begin on B *fa* for the eighth [*ton*]. That is the difference between the
two *tons*. Here is the first fugue.

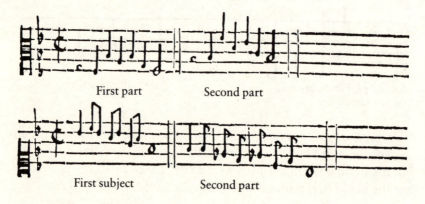

First part          Second part

First subject          Second part

72 In this instance Denis may have meant to refer to the fifth *ton* rather than the sixth.
   According to his earlier statements, it is the fifth *ton* whose dominant is on C *sol, ut, fa*;
   the dominant of the sixth *ton* is specified as A *mi, la, re* (p. 85).

92

That is all I have been able to discover and observe regarding the extent of all the *tons*. The organist is to be advised that for those in religious orders, since many voices in their choirs can sing higher than parish singers, he should play the eighth *ton* on G *re, sol, ut*, with B♮[73] and also the third *ton* on A *mi, la, re*, with B♭.

73 Instead of on F as specified in the previous chapter.

# Treatise on fugues,
# and how they should be realized [II]

Now I must demonstrate how many kinds of fugues there are and how they should be treated. Father Parran has written a treatise on music in which he states that there are only three kinds of fugues,[74] in which he is correct where vocal music is concerned. But in instrumental music, and particularly for the organ, there are four kinds, as you will be able to see in what follows.

The first is the simple fugue, like those presented above in all the *tons*. The second is the double fugue, which is called double because two subjects[75] must be played in contrary motion, one together with the other. Once the two subjects have been undertaken in the first place, they must be continued and played together throughout, as you can see in the example that follows.

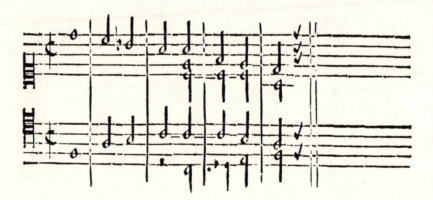

74 Antoine Parran, *Traité de la musique théorique et pratique* (Paris, 1639), p. 95. Examples of the three kinds of fugues, each in four parts, appear on pp. 107–11.
75 At this point and in other places in the two chapters on fugue, Denis employs the word 'fugue' where 'subject' is apparently meant. For the sake of clarity in these instances, 'subject' has been substituted in the English translation.

This fugue is difficult and not especially pleasing, because of the two parts that must be made to sound together at all times, and it is very troublesome.[76]

The third fugue is the inverted fugue [*fugue renversée*], which is much more beautiful and easier to execute than the preceding, for while the previous fugue proceeds with two subjects at once, in this one it is only necessary that one [subject] be made to follow after the other, as you can see in this example.

First part                          Second part

The fourth fugue is the continuous fugue [*fugue continuë*]. This fugue is proper only for the organ, since in vocal music it cannot be realized, especially when there is text. But it could be done quite well in the event that there were no words.

The nature of the continuous fugue must be understood. After the fugue has begun and the first voice has stated the subject, it must be heard in some other voice. As soon as it has been completed in one voice, another voice must state it. Thus the voices must always follow closely, one after the other. Do nothing at all between two statements,[77] for it would not be a continuous fugue if that were allowed, and [the subject] must always be heard from the beginning to the end. That is why it is called the continuous fugue, and I have never heard it played and worked out so well as by Monsieur Bienvenu, who is the one who taught me music and organ playing. The subject must be quite short and must have only four or five notes. An episode could indeed be fashioned in the middle of the piece, but only for a measure at the most; then take up the subject

---

76 An example of a double fugue in four parts appears on pp. 54–5 of the *Traité de la composition* of Nivers. Nivers's rules for fugue (pp. 49–51) are an informative adjunct to Denis's comments.
77 In other words, there should be no extended episodes.

again immediately.[78] There you have all that can be said concerning the four principal fugues.

Here is another piece which is quite beautiful and quite unusual. I do not know what I ought to call it because there is no obligation to pursue any one subject, meaning that all the subjects are different. In order to illustrate this clearly we must take up the plainchant of the hymn of Saint John the Baptist, in which there are six syllables that represent the six monosyllables of music, which we shall use to demonstrate how this piece should be executed. First, it must be understood that the first subject must be taken from the plainchant, which is *Ut queant laxis*, with *Resonare fibris* as the second subject, as in the plainchant. The third subject will be *Mira gestorum*, and the fourth *Famuli tuorum*, like the plainchant. Thus have four voices entered, making four different subjects. Two subjects remain to be played, *Solve polluti* and *Labii reatum*, which the organist will be at liberty to place in whichever voice he wishes, making them sound the plainchant like the others. Four notes remain to complete the verset, where there is *Sancte Joannes*. Here the organist should play pedal points on each note or else play a continuous fugue, as Monsieur Titelouze did it in his Book of Hymns.[79]

This sort of verse is very pleasing to realize and hear but is very infrequently employed, for there are many who do not understand it and do not have the skill for it. An organist who listened, unaware of the player's intention, might summarily declare that here was an incompetent organist who was not following his subject, [the listener] not having the expertise to recognize the player's intent.

There you have all that I have been able to discover and observe concerning *tons* and fugues, in the interest of providing knowledge to those who wish to learn and satisfaction to the experts, who will have the pleasure of deciding whether I have done well. Those who aspire to mastery can profit therefrom, and will be grateful to me.

78 Specific references to this form by other French theorists are few. Salomon de Caus gives two completely notated examples of a form he refers to as '*fugue continue*', along with instructions for composing such pieces. These examples are in fact canons at the unison and fifth. See Salomon de Caus, *Institution harmonique* (Frankfurt, 1615), Part II, pp. 39–41. Denis may be referring to canon, or merely describing an imitative technique for handling a relatively short subject; cf. the five fugues on a single theme by D'Anglebert (*Pièces de clavessin*).

79 Titelouze, *Hymnes de l'Eglise*, pp. 34–9. For more on the *Ut queant laxis* hymn and its possibly direct connection to Guido d'Arezzo, see Andrew Hughes, 'Solmization' (I), *The New Grove*, vol. xvii, pp. 458–9.

# The proper manner of playing the harpsichord and the organ

A philosopher used to tell his disciples that he was like the whetstone, which does not cut, but makes cutting possible; one might say the same thing about me. It could be said, 'He wishes to teach, which he should not do, for there are others who are better prepared to undertake this than he, and who play the harpsichord far better than he'. Yet it does not follow that since I do not play as well [as they], that I therefore cannot clearly explain how to play correctly, or prescribe proper hand position, which is the foundation of good playing. For I am well aware that there are those who play better than I, but they are few in number, and they do not wish to trouble themselves with writing.

There are some masters who have their pupils place their hands in such a way that the wrist is lower than the hand, which is very bad, and properly speaking, a vice, because the hand no longer possesses strength. Others make one hold the wrist higher than the hand, which is a fault because the fingers then resemble sticks, straight and stiff. For the proper position of the hand, the wrist and the hand must be at the same height; in other words, the wrist must be at the same height as the large knuckle of the fingers.[80] When I began to study, the masters invariably said never to play with the thumb of the right hand.[81] But I have since realized that even if one had as

---

80 The result of such a positioning of the wrist may be noted in 'The Music Master' by Jan Steen (ca. 1660), reproduced in the article 'Harpsichord', *The New Grove* vol. viii, p. 225.

81 This statement should not be taken to mean that the thumb was *never* used, but rather that most figurations and passagework were played with the central fingers of the right hand. The published works of Titelouze, which contain repertoire representative of the time during which Denis 'began to study', show many notes for the right hand that could only have been played by the thumb (as in octaves, for example). Little is known of French keyboard fingering practice in the first half of the seventeenth century, but based on the fingerings published in 1665 by Nivers (*Livre d'orgue*, Preface), the fingerings employed in France during those earlier years may well have been similar to fingerings known to have been in use in England, Germany, Spain, and Italy. See Peter le Huray, 'Fingering, Keyboard, to c. 1650', *The New Grove*, vol. vi, pp. 567–70.

many hands as Briareus[82] one would use them all, even though there are not that many keys on the keyboard.

After hand position I must speak of mordents [*pincements*], *fredons*,[83] and cadential trills [*cadences parfaites*]. Mordents are made according to the value of the notes, and as a result there are two kinds of mordents: the single, which has the value of an eighth note, and the double, which has the value of a quarter note. The *fredon* has the value of a half note, without being closed and terminated like the cadential trill. Finally there is the cadential trill, which is closed and concluded completely.

There are those who err greatly, especially when they begin a fugue. For whatever note the fugue may begin on, they play a mordent as long as the value of the note, which is a serious error. For example, if a fugue begins on G *re, sol, ut*, they play an alternation of G and A, making it as long as the value of the note. No one can judge whether the intention is to start on G or A, and thus the first note of the fugue cannot be determined. Now in order to guard against this mistake, you should be advised that no organist begins a fugue with a mordent unless the mordent is but half the value of the note with which the fugue begins, so that the other half of the note is held, making it clear that this is the note with which he means to start. To begin a fugue properly, one should play the first note and strike its neighbor as well, releasing the latter and holding the one that should sound.[84] Regarding the graces of organ playing

82 A giant in Greek mythology, son of Uranus and Gaea, Briareus is described as having 50 heads and 100 arms. See Homer, *Iliad*, I, lines 400–4.

83 The term *fredon* seems to have been little used in French treatises of the seventeenth and eighteenth centuries. In Cotgrave's *Dictionarie of the French and English Tongues* (London, 1611), *fredon* is defined as 'a semie-quaver, or semie-semie-quaver, in Musicke; and hence, Division . . . ', and the corresponding verb *fredonner* is defined as meaning 'to shake, divide, warble, quaver in singing, or playing on an instrument'. In the *Encyclopédie ou Dictionnaire raisonné* of Denis Diderot and Jean d'Alembert (Paris, 1751–8, vol. vii, p. 293), *fredon* is defined thus: 'An old-fashioned musical term that signifies a *passage rapide*, almost always diatonic, of many notes on the same syllable. It is close to what has come to be called a *roulade*, the difference being that the *roulade* is written, whereas the *fredon* is ordinarily an addition of taste that the singer applies to the note.'

84 A similar technique for playing mordents is described in at least two earlier sources. In the 'Fundamentum' of Hans Buchner (ca. 1520) is found the following: 'Remember, therefore, that the notes which have the curved lines are called mordents [*mordentes*], and observe that two notes must always be struck at once, namely the one marked with the curved line with the middle finger, and the nearest lower neighbor with the index finger which, however, is quickly withdrawn, as if in a tremor.' Tomás de Sancta María also

[*animations du toucher de l'orgue*] they are similar to shadows in painting.[85] Just as the painter must take great care that the shadows, which he introduces to bring out the form and the relief, do not create a blur that offends the eye, so must the organist take care not to shake and wriggle his fingers so much that he creates confusion, and a blur that prevents one from hearing the harmonies and the rhythms.[86] For he who performs mordents, trills, *fredons*, and cadential ornaments well and in the right places is bound to be considered quite expert.

If there are four consecutive notes, one must be careful to play mordents on only two of them. That is to say, if you play a mordent on the first one, it is proper to play one on the third as well, and not on the second or the last. And if you wish to play a mordent on the second, it is proper to play one on the fourth as well, and not on the first or the third; otherwise there would be confusion and blurring. Only rarely should mordents be played on eighth notes that are in passagework; if the notes descend, one should play mordents to the upper [notes], and if they ascend one should play mordents to the lower [notes], ornamenting every other note as I have mentioned above.[87]

describes a similar technique in his treatise *Libro llamado arte de tañer fantasia* (Valladolid, 1565, fol. 49[r]).

85 Denis may have borrowed this image from the Preface to the *Hymnes de l'Eglise* of Titelouze (p. 4), where it is used in reference to the employment of dissonance. The same image is also invoked by de La Voye-Mignot in reference to dissonance (*Traité de musique*, p. 70).

86 *mouvements*. This expression often carries the meaning of 'tempi' in later French theoretical writings, but here it appears to be used to refer to rhythm. Mersenne presents tables of musical examples that relate notes in various rhythmic patterns ('*mouvemens rythmiques*') to the metric feet of verse. See *Harmonie universelle*, vol. II, *Livre sixiesme de l'art de bien chanter*, pp. 376, 408–9.

87 The employment of single or double mordents in ascending and descending lines had already been described in several sources. The earlier authors are generally in agreement with Denis regarding the employment of the upper auxiliary in descending lines and the lower auxiliary in ascending lines. Sancta María refers to the single-mordent types as *quiebros senzillos*, states that they are usually played on quarter notes, and gives many examples of their use on alternate notes in ascending and descending melodic figures (*Libro llamado arte de tañer fantasia*, fol. 46[v]–47[r], 50[r]–51[v]). According to Sancta María, *quiebros* played on weak beats are 'more elegant'. In the *Orgel oder Instrument Tabulatur* (Leipzig, 1571, fol. 11[v]), Elias Nikolaus Ammerbach illustrates two double-mordent types, which he styles 'ascendendo' and 'descendendo'; these are also shown in examples where they are employed in a manner consistent with Denis's rules. According to Ammerbach, 'Mordents [*mordanten*] are made when a note is mingled with its neighbor, and when correctly employed they lend much charm and grace to melodies.' Compare also the *tremoli* of Girolamo Diruta (*Il Transilvano*, Part I, 10[r]–11[r])

It is wonderful to behold a person who plays well and gracefully, and whose hand is correctly positioned. But one must be very careful not to play with either force or tension, for he who is tense or strained in his hands or in his body will never play well. That is why the masters who teach should carefully consider the ability of the person who is being taught: whether he is capable of playing according to the rules, and whether his fingers can do so. For if it is wished that a person play the cadential trill with the last two fingers and these fingers cannot do so without strain, he should be allowed to play this trill with the first two fingers[88] and cut it off subtly with the second finger, as I do. If I had sought to compel myself to do it as it is supposed to be done, I would never have played the harpsichord or the organ well.

and the *tremoletti* of Michael Praetorius (*Syntagma Musicum*, vol. III, p. 235). Such ornaments, says Praetorius, are employed by organists and harpsichordists more often than by singers.

The mordent to the upper auxiliary is not included in the ornament tables of Nivers and D'Anglebert, nor does it appear among the numerous written-out ornaments found in the unmeasured preludes of Louis Couperin.

88 It is likely that Denis means the index and middle fingers.

# On bad habits that occur among those who play instruments

Since I am an instrument maker, I am obliged to receive all sorts of persons in my shop. Some come to see and hear my products, others come to buy, and thus I have the pleasure of seeing all sorts of people play, and of witnessing all the grimaces[89] and postures that are affected. Many people are not careful about these things, and the masters who instruct cannot be observing very well, as their students must be doing as they are taught. I, however, note everything but tell them nothing. I used to speak freely to them, but I realized that some of them took it ill, so I have restrained myself from taking this great liberty, and I have decided to do my speaking on paper. Perhaps people will not be so readily offended by this as by the spoken word.

Sometimes a foppish young man will come to me to request a good harpsichord or spinet. Thinking to perform marvels, he is more careful to turn his head, to see whether I appreciate what he is playing, than he is to pay attention to what he is doing. And to make himself heard, he makes more noise beating time[90] with his foot

---

89 In *L'Art de toucher le clavecin* (Paris, 1717, p. 4), François Couperin recommends the following: 'With regard to facial grimaces, one can cure one's self of these by placing a mirror on the music stand of the spinet or harpsichord.'

90 *la mesure*. This term cannot be translated as 'measure'; it referred instead to the musical pulse. The expression is defined by Salomon de Caus: 'In beginning a song, whichever it might be, the hand must be held up, then lowered, then raised again, always in the same proportion, as long as the song lasts. This lowering and raising is called *Mesure*, of which there are ordinarily two sorts . . . ' Descriptions follow of *Mesure Double* and *Mesure Triple* (*Institution harmonique*, Part II, pp. 5–6). Mersenne relates the *mesure* to various note values: 'For example, the whole note ordinarily lasts one raising and one lowering of the hand . . . the half note . . . one raising or one lowering, and the quarter note one half of a raising or lowering . . . The lowering or striking is twice as long as the raising in ternary time . . . ' (*Harmonie universelle*, vol. II, *Livre cinquiesme de la composition*, p. 324). Mersenne also makes note of the following practice: 'Those who now lead ensembles mark the *mesure* by moving the necks of the lutes or theorbos that they play . . . ' (*Harmonie universelle*, vol. II, *Livre cinquiesme de la composition*, p. 324ᵛ). Writing in 1656, de La Voye-Mignot observes that the *mesure* is sometimes kept by beating the foot, the hand, or an object (such as the supposedly fatal baton of Lully), while at other times it is kept 'mentally' (*Traité de musique*, p. 11).

than does the instrument he is playing. Others behave much more comically, playing half of a trill in the air and the rest on the instrument.[91] Others swing their heads at every moment, with a groan that is rather amusing.

I once saw a young man who played very well, and at every third beat he made a click with his tongue, so loudly that I could hardly keep myself from laughing. There is an organist who plays the organ and the harpsichord quite well, though he is by no means an organist of Paris. When he wishes to play something which he thinks he plays well, he flings both his legs to one side and sets his body awry, with a scowl on his face, which is nearly unbearable to those who watch him play.

I have written down all the above things in order to warn those who are already accustomed to these imperfections that they should be aware of them, and to warn masters who teach that they should be careful that their students do not acquire bad habits.

## THE END

---

91 Denis is perhaps referring to those who attempted, with various motions and mannerisms, to compensate for inadequate technique.

# Appendix A

A COMPARISON OF PARALLEL PASSAGES FROM THE PUBLISHED
WRITINGS OF JEAN DENIS AND MARIN MERSENNE

The passages quoted from the *Traité* of Denis appeared in both the 1643 and
1650 editions. Minor typographical errors have been corrected without
comment.

M. Mersenne, *Nouvelles observations physiques et mathematiques* (Paris, ca.
1638), p. 22.

Il est certain que les premiers Claviers n'ont eu que les 8 sons, & les 7
intervalles de la main harmonique de Guy Aretin, suivant les lettres A, B, C, D,
E, F, G, *a*, dont j'ay parlé dans la premiere Prop. du 6 livre des Consonances,
& souvent ailleurs; d'où il est arrivé que les feintes, ou dieses qui du depuis y
ont esté ajoûtées, ont retenu le nom des marches principales, dont elles sont
comme des dépendences, ou des supplémens: car la feinte éloignée d'un demiton mineur de C *ut*, est nommée la feinte de C *sol ut*, & ainsi des autres qui sont
marquées du signe de diese dans la Musique pratique des notes, quoy que
plusieurs marquent la feinte ou le *fa* d'*E mi la*, par le *b mol*, aussi bien que celle
de *b fa b mi*, parce que ces 2 feintes ont les mesmes proprietez. Quant à la feinte
de *F ut*, & *G re*, elles se marquent comme celle de C *ut*.

J. Denis, *Traité de l'accord de l'espinette* (Paris, 1643 and 1650), original pp.
7–8.

Ils ont commencé à faire un Clavier, sçavoir des touches sans feintes ou diezes;
& pour preuves, les feintes & diezes n'ont point de propres syllabes que celles
qu'elles empruntent des touches: Pour exemple le *C sol, ut, fa*, a une feinte qui
est nommée la feinte de *C sol, ut, fa*; celle de *E mi, la*, porte son nom d'elle-
mesme, pource qu'en *E mi, la*, la touche, il ne se trouve point de *fa*, qui est le
nom de la feinte, elle est marquée, comme celle de *B fa, b mi*, & a toutes ses
proprietez pareilles, & sont marquées ainsi tous deux ♭, & toutes les autres
sont marquées ainsi ♯, une en *F ut, fa*, & une en *G ré, sol, ut*.

M. Mersenne, *Nouvelles observations*, p. 22.

Or quelques-uns s'imaginent que les premiers Inventeurs de ces feintes
accorderent premierement toutes les Quintes iustes, ou quasi iustes, suivant
l'accord égal, dont j'ay parlé dans l'Observation precedente; mais que leur

oreille ne pouvant supporter les Tierces majeures (qui sont necessairement trop fortes, à raison que tous les demitons estans égaux, & comme moyens entre le demiton majeur & le mineur, chacun de ces demitons est trop grand pour changer la Tierce mineure en majeure) ils tempererent tellement l'accord, qu'ils affoiblirent les Quintes pour baisser les Tierces majeures, qui blessoient l'ouye par leur trop grande rudesse. Ce qu'ils ont fait avec une telle adresse, qu'ils ont douze Quintes si peu affoiblies & diminuées, qu'elles ne blessent point l'oreille; dont la premiere est depuis la feinte d'*E mi*, qu'on tient forte, iusques à celle de *b fa*: la seconde est de *b fa* forte contre F fa . . . La derniere Quinte est de la feinte de *G re* au *fa* d'*E mi*, auquel se rencontre le defaut de l'accord . . .

J. Denis, *Traité de l'accord de l'espinette*, pp. 9–11.

. . . comme nos Anciens voulurent accorder l'Espinette, ayant composé le Clavier dans sa perfection, comme il est maintenant, ils accorderent, comme j'ay dit cy-devant, innocemment toutes les quintes iustes, qui est l'accord que cét homme nous presente, & venant à toucher, ils trouverent que cét accord repugnoit fort à leurs esperances, & que les tierces maieures estoient trop fortes, & si rudes que l'oreille ne les pouvoit souffrir, & qu'ils ne trouvoient point de semitons ny maieurs ny mineurs, mais un semi-ton moyen, qui n'est ny maieur ny mineur, estant plus foible que le maieur & plus fort que le mineur; & que les cadences ne valoient rien, ne pouvant souffrir cette rudesse qui blessoit si fort le sens de l'oüye, qui donne le plus de plaisir à nostre ame; se resolurent de temperer si bien cét accord, que l'oreille fust aussi contente de la Musique Instrumentale, que de la Vocale: Et voulant baisser les tierces majeures, se trouva que par necessité il falloit baisser toutes les quintes & les temperer en sorte que l'oreille le peut souffrir . . . sur la quantite des quintes qui sont douze en tout . . . & la premiere corde est la feinte de *E mi, la*, & sa quinte *B fa*, qu'il faut tenir foible, & de la feinte *B fa*, à la touche *F ut, fa*, qu'il faut encore tenir foible, & ainsi des autres, comme la Pratique nous enseigne; & la derniere corde est la feinte de *G ré, sol, ut*, qui est la fin de l'accord.

M. Mersenne, *Nouvelles observations*, p. 23.

. . . & le ton superflu de 2 demitons majeurs, lesquels se trouvent aux 2 touches qui n'ont point de feinte, à sçavoir en *D re* & *A la*, qui ont le demiton majeur des deux costez; au lieu que toutes les autres touches ont la feinte du demiton mineur pour servir à la chromatique . . .

J. Denis, *Traité de l'accord de l'espinette*, p. 11.

. . . & le ton superflu est composé de deux semi-tons majeurs . . . & se rencontre en deux endroicts qui sont aux deux touches qui n'ont point de feintes sçavoir en *D la, ré, sol*, & en *A mi, la, ré*, qui ont des deux costez un semi-ton majeur, & toutes les autres touches ont une feinte d'un semi-ton mineur qui est le semi-ton qui ne sert qu'à la Cromatique.

# Appendix A

M. Mersenne, *Nouvelles observations*, p. 23.

Or bien que les Praticiens trouvent l'accord d'égalité fort rude, à raison de l'excez des Tierces majeures, & de la diminution des demitons, qui diminuent la fermeté & la bonté des cadences, qui ne valent aussi rien sur les demitons mineurs; & qu'ils iugent plus à propos d'accommoder tellement les touches du Luth & de la Viole, par le moyen du monochorde, qu'ils soient parfaitement d'accord avec l'Epinette, que de corrompre & destruire leur accord, dont ils trouvent l'harmonie plus douce; & qu'il ne soit pas si malaisé de mettre lesdites touches sur le manche du Luth, (soit avec des touches d'yvoire, ou en usant de ressorts cachez dedans ou dessous le manche) . . .

J. Denis, *Traité de l'accord de l'espinette*, pp. 12–13.

Je luy dis qu'il avoit mauvaise raison de vouloir gaster le bon & parfait accord pour l'accommoder à des Instruments imparfaits, & qu'il falloit plustost chercher la perfection du Luth & de la Viole, & trouver le moyen de faire que les semi-tons fussent majeures & mineurs, comme nous les avons sur l'Espinette, ce qui ne se peut faire avec les touches des cordes dont on touche les Luths, pource qu'il faudroit qu'elles fussent faites en pieds de mousches; ce qui se peut faire par le moyen des touches d'yvoire, que l'on peut mettre par le compas & par la proportion du Monochorde, & par ce moyen on accordera le Luth & la Viole, avec l'Espinette, dans l'accord musical & harmonique.

# Appendix B

A TRANSCRIPTION OF THE '*PRELUDE* FOR DETERMINING
WHETHER THE TUNING IS GOOD THROUGHOUT'

* G♭ in the original.

# Bibliography

## SIXTEENTH-, SEVENTEENTH-, AND EIGHTEENTH-CENTURY SOURCES

Aaron, Pietro. *Lucidario in musica*. Venice: Girolamo Scotto, 1545.

*Toscanello de la musica*. Venice: Bernardino and Matheo de Vitali, 1523; facsimile edition, New York: Broude Brothers, 1969; trans. of the 1529 edition, Peter Bergquist. Colorado Springs: Colorado College Music Press, 1970.

Ammerbach, Elias Nikolaus. *Orgel oder Instrument Tabulatur*. Leipzig: Jacob Berwalds Erben, 1571; second edition, 1583; modern edition, including facsimile, ed. Charles Jacobs. Oxford: Clarendon Press, 1984.

Anglebert, Jean-Henry D'. *Pièces de clavessin*. Paris: author, 1689; facsimile edition, New York: Broude Brothers, 1965; modern edition, ed. Kenneth Gilbert (including works from manuscript sources). Paris: Heugel, 1975.

Angleria, Camillo. *La regola del contraponto e della musical compositione*. Milan: Giorgio Rolla, 1622; facsimile edition, Bologna: Forni Editore, 1983.

Attaingnant, Pierre, ed. *Magnificat sur les huit tons avec Te deum laudamus et deux preludes*, Paris, 1530; *Tablature pour le jeu dorgues espinetes et manicordions sur le plain chant de Cunctipotens et Kyrie fons*, Paris, 1531; modern edition, ed. Yvonne Rokseth. Paris: Publications de la Société Française de Musicologie (Heugel), 1931; second edition, 1967.

Bacilly, Bénigne de. *Remarques curieuses sur l'art de bien chanter*. Paris: C. Blageart, 1668; facsimile of the 1679 edition, Geneva: Minkoff Reprint, 1974; trans. and ed. Austin Caswell as *A Commentary upon the Art of Proper Singing*. Brooklyn, New York: Institute of Mediaeval Music, 1968.

Banchieri, Adriano. *Cartella musicale*. Venice: Giacomo Vincenti, 1614; facsimile edition, Bologna: Forni Editore, 1968; trans. Clifford Cranna. Unpublished dissertation, Stanford University, 1981.

*Conclusioni nel suono dell'organo*. Bologna: Heirs of Giovanni Rossi, 1609; facsimile edition, Milan: Bollettino, 1934; facsimile edition, Bologna: Forni Editore, 1968; facsimile edition, New York: Broude Brothers, 1975; trans. Lee Garrett. Colorado Springs: Colorado College Music Press, 1982.

*L'organo suonarino*. Venice: Ricciardo Amadino, 1605; facsimile edition, Introduction by Giulio Cattin. Amsterdam: Frits Knuf, 1969; trans. Donald Marcase. Unpublished dissertation, Indiana University, 1970.

# Bibliography

Bendeler, Johann Philipp. *Organopoeia*. Quedlinburg: Theodore Calvisius, ca. 1690; facsimile edition, Afterword by Rudolf Bruhin. Amsterdam: Frits Knuf, 1972.

Bermudo, Juan. *Libro llamado declaración de instrumentos musicales*. Osuna: Juan de León, 1555; facsimile edition, Afterword by Santiago Kastner. Kassel: Bärenreiter, 1957.

Boyvin, Jacques. *Premier livre d'orgue*. Paris: author, 1689. *Second livre d'orgue*. Paris: Christophe Ballard, 1700; modern edition, ed. Alexandre Guilmant and André Pirro. Paris: A. Durand et Fils, 1905; reprinted 1972.

Brossard, Sébastien de. *Dictionaire de musique*. Paris: Christophe Ballard, 1703; facsimile of the 1705 second edition, Introduction by Harald Heckmann. Hilversum, Netherlands: Frits Knuf, 1965; trans. Albion Gruber. Henryville, Pennsylvania: Institute of Mediaeval Music, 1982; facsimile of the 1708 third edition, Geneva: Minkoff Reprint, 1985.

Buchner, Hans. 'Fundamentum' (ca. 1520). MS Zürich: Zentralbibliothek, Codex 284; MS Basel: Öffentliche Bibliothek der Universität, F. I. 8a; modern edition: *Hans Buchner, Sämtliche Orgelwerke*, ed. Jost Harro Schmidt. Frankfurt: Henry Litolff, 1974.

Caus, Salomon de. *Institution harmonique divisée en deux parties*. Frankfurt: Jan Norton, 1615; facsimile edition, Preface by Pierre Féruselle. Geneva: Minkoff Reprint, 1980.

*Les raisons des forces mouvantes*. Frankfurt: Jan Norton, 1615; reissued Paris: Charles Sevestre, 1624. [*Livre troisiesme traitant de la fabrique des orgues*]

Chales, Claude François Milliet de. *Cursus seu mundus mathematicus*. Lyons: Anisson, 1674. [vol. III, Tractatus XXII: *Musica*]

Chambonnières, Jacques Champion de. *Pièces de clavessin*. 2 vols. Paris: author, 1670; facsimile edition, Paris: Éditions Maurice Senart, 1925; reprinted New York: Broude Brothers, 1967; modern edition, ed. Thurston Dart. Monaco: Éditions de l'Oiseau-Lyre, 1969.

*Oeuvres complètes*. Ed. Paul Brunold and André Tessier (from printed and manuscript sources). Paris: Éditions Maurice Senart, 1925; reprint edition, trans. Denise Restout. New York: Broude Brothers, 1967.

Charpentier, Marc-Antoine. 'Règles de composition' (ca. 1692–8, with additional manuscript notes by Loulié or Brossard). MS Paris: Bibliothèque Nationale Mss. fr. nouv. acq. 6350, 6355; transcribed Clarence Barber in 'The Liturgical Music of Marc-Antoine Charpentier'. Unpublished dissertation, Harvard University, 1955; trans. Lillian Ruff, 'M.-A. Charpentier's "Règles de composition"', *The Consort* xxiv (1967), 233–70.

Chaumont, Lambert. *Pièces d'orgue sur les 8 tons*. Huy: Georges Libert, 1695; modern edition, ed. Charles Hens and Roger Bragard. Liège: Éditions Dynamo, 1939; modern edition, ed. Jean Ferrard. Paris: Heugel, 1970.

Corneille, Thomas. *Le dictionnaire des arts et des sciences*. Paris: veuve de J.-B. Coignard, 1694.

# Bibliography

Corrette, Michel. *Le maitre de clavecin pour l'accompagnement*. Paris: author, 1753; facsimile edition, Geneva: Minkoff Reprint, 1976.

*Les amusemens du Parnasse; methode courte et facile pour apprendre à toucher le clavecin*. Paris: author, 1749.

Costeley, Guillaume. *Musique*. Paris: Adrian Le Roy and Robert Ballard, 1570; modern edition, ed. Henry Expert. Paris: Alphonse Leduc, 1896.

Cotgrave, Randle. *A Dictionarie of the French and English Tongues*. London: Adam Islip, 1611; facsimile edition, Introduction by William S. Woods. Columbia, South Carolina: University of South Carolina Press, 1950.

Couperin, François. *L'Art de toucher le clavecin*. Paris: author, 1716; rev. 1717; facsimile edition, New York: Broude Brothers, 1969; facsimile edition, Geneva: Minkoff reprint, 1985; trans. and ed. Margery Halford. Port Washington, New York: Alfred Publishing, 1974.

Couperin, Louis. *Pièces de clavecin*. Ed. Paul Brunold. Monaco: Éditions de l'Oiseau-Lyre, 1936; rev. Thurston Dart, 1959; rev. Davitt Moroney, 1985.

*Pièces de clavecin*. Ed. Alan Curtis. Paris: Heugel, 1970.

Cousu, Antoine de. *La musique universelle, contenant toute la pratique et toute la théorie*. Paris: Robert Ballard, 1658; facsimile edition (incomplete), Geneva: Minkoff Reprint, 1972.

Denis, Jean (II). *Traité de l'accord de l'espinette*. Paris: author, 1643; rev. second edition, Paris: Robert Ballard, 1650; facsimile edition, Introduction by Alan Curtis. New York: Da Capo Press, 1969.

Descartes, René. *Compendium musicae* [written in 1618]. Utrecht: Zyll and Ackersdijck, 1650; second edition, Amsterdam: Johannes Jansson, Jr., 1656; trans. of 1656 edition Walter Robert, Introduction and Notes by Charles Kent. Rome: American Institute of Musicology, 1961.

Diderot, Denis and Jean d'Alembert. *Encyclopédie ou Dictionnaire raisonné des sciences, des arts, et des métiers*. 28 vols. Paris, 1751–8; facsimile edition, Stuttgart: Friedrich Frommann Verlag, 1966.

Diruta, Girolamo. *Il Transilvano*. Venice: Giacomo Vincenti, 1593; *Seconda parte del Transilvano*. Venice: Giacomo Vincenti, 1609; facsimile edition of both volumes, Bologna: Forni Editore, 1969; facsimile edition of both volumes, Introduction by Edward Soehnlen and Murray Bradshaw. Buren, Netherlands: Frits Knuf, 1983; trans. Edward Soehnlen and Murray Bradshaw. Henryville, Pennsylvania: Institute of Mediaeval Music, forthcoming.

Furetière, Antoine. *Dictionnaire universel*. 2 vols. The Hague and Rotterdam: Arnout & Reinier Leers, 1690; facsimile edition, 3 vols., Introduction by Alain Rey. Paris: S.N.L. – Le Robert, 1978.

Gaffurius, Franchinus. *Practica musice*. Milan: Guillermus Signerre, 1496; facsimile edition, New York: Broude Brothers, 1979.

Geoffroy, Jean-Nicolas [attrib.]. 'Livre des pieces de clavessin de tous les tons naturels et transposéz' (copied ca. 1695). MS Paris: Bibliothèque Nationale, Rés. 475.

Gigault, Nicolas. *Livre de musique dédié à la Trés Saincte Vierge*. Paris:

author, 1683. *Livre de musique pour l'orgue*. Paris: author, 1685; modern edition, ed. Alexandre Guilmant and André Pirro. Paris: A. Durand et Fils, 1902.

Gomboust, Jacques. *Plan de Paris, dressé géometriquement en 1649, et publiée en 1652*; reprinted Paris: Société des Bibliophiles françois, 1858.

Huygens, Constantin. *Correspondance et oeuvres musicales de Constantin Huygens (Musique et musiciens au XVII<sup>e</sup> siècle)*, ed. W. J. A. Jonckbloet and J. P. N. Land. Leyden: E. J. Brill, 1882.

Jullien, Gilles. *Premier livre d'orgue*. Paris: Henry Lesclop, 1690; modern edition, ed. Norbert Dufourcq. Paris: Heugel, 1952.

Laborde, Jean-Benjamin de. *Essai sur la musique ancienne et moderne*. 4 vols. Paris: Philippe-Denys Pierres, 1780.

La Rousselière, Jean-Baptiste-Charles de. *Traitté des languettes impérialles pour la perfection du clavecin*. Paris: author, 1679; facsimile edition, Geneva: Minkoff Reprint, 1972.

La Voye-Mignot, de [first name unknown]. *Traité de la musique*. Paris: Robert Ballard, 1656; trans. and ed. Albion Gruber. Brooklyn, New York: The Institute of Mediaeval Music, Ltd., 1972; facsimile of the 1666 second edition, Geneva: Minkoff Reprint, 1972.

Lebègue, Nicolas. *Les pièces de clavessin*. Paris: author, 1677. *Second livre de clavessin*. Paris: author, 1687; modern edition, ed. Norbert Dufourcq. Monaco: Éditions de l'Oiseau-Lyre, 1956.

*Les pièces d'orgue*. Paris: author, 1676. *Second livre d'orgue*. Paris: author, 1678. *Troisième livre d'orgue*. Paris: author, 1685; modern edition, ed. Alexandre Guilmant and André Pirro. Paris: A. Durand et Fils, 1909.

Le Gallois, Jean. 'Lettre de Monsieur Le Gallois à Mademoiselle Regnault de Solier touchant la musique'. Paris: E. Michallet and G. Quinet, 1680; facsimile edition, Geneva: Minkoff Reprint, 1984; partially transcribed and translated by David Fuller in 'French harpsichord playing in the 17th century – after le Gallois', *Early Music* iv (1976), 22–6.

*Livre d'orgue* [late seventeenth century, anon., formerly attributed to Jean-Nicolas Geoffroy]. MS Paris: Bibliothèque Nationale, Rés. 476; modern edition, ed. Jean Bonfils. Paris: Heugel, 1974.

Loulié, E. *Eléments ou principes de musique*. Paris: Christophe Ballard, 1696; trans. and ed. Albert Cohen. Brooklyn, New York: Institute of Mediaeval Music, 1965; facsimile edition, Geneva: Minkoff Reprint, 1971.

Maillart, Pierre. *Les tons, ou discours, sur les modes de musique, et les tons de l'église, et la distinction en iceux*. Tournai: Charles Martin, 1610; facsimile edition, Geneva: Minkoff Reprint, 1972.

*Manière de toucher lorgue dans toute la propreté et la delicatesse quie est en usage aujourdhy à Paris*. Anonymous MS Paris: Bibliothèque de l'Arsenal, ms. 3042, fols. 100–9; transcribed by William Pruitt in 'Un traité d'interpretation du XVII<sup>e</sup> siècle', *L'Orgue* clii (1974), 99–111.

*Manuscrit Bauyn* (ca. 1690). MS Paris: Bibliothèque Nationale, Rés. Vm$^7$ 674–5; facsimile edition, ed. François Lesure. Geneva: Minkoff Reprint, 1977.

# Bibliography

Masson, Charles. *Nouveau traité des règles pour la composition de la musique.* Paris: Christophe Ballard, 1697; facsimile of the 1699 second edition, Introduction by Imogene Horsley. New York: Da Capo Press, 1967; facsimile of the 1705 third edition. Geneva: Minkoff Reprint, 1971.

Merlin, François. 'Recherche de plusiers singularités'. MS Paris: F/Pn Ms. Fr. 9152.

Mersenne, Marin. *Cogitata physico-mathematica.* Paris: Antoine Bertier, 1644.

*Correspondance du P. Marin Mersenne,* ed. Cornelius de Waard *et al.* 15 vols. Paris: Presses Universitaires de France, 1945–83.

*Les preludes de l'harmonie universelle ou Questions curieuses.* Paris: Henry Guenon, 1634.

*Harmonie universelle.* Paris: Sébastien Cramoisy and Pierre Ballard, 1636–7; facsimile edition of the author's copy, with his marginal annotations. 3 vols. Introduction by François Lesure. Paris: Éditions du Centre National de la Recherche Scientifique, 1963; vol. II trans. Roger Chapman. The Hague: Martinus Nijhoff, 1957.

*Nouvelles observations physiques et mathematiques.* Paris, ca. 1638; facsimile edition appended to vol. III of the *Harmonie universelle.*

*Questions harmoniques.* Paris: Jacques Villery, 1633.

Millet, Jean. *La belle methode, ou l'art de bien chanter.* Lyons: Jean Gregoire, 1666; facsimile edition, Introduction by Albert Cohen. New York: Da Capo Press, 1973.

Montfort, Blockland de. *Instruction méthodique et fort facile pour apprendre la musique practique.* Lyons: Jean de Tournes, 1587; facsimile edition, Geneva: Minkoff Reprint, 1972.

MS London, British Museum Add. Ms. 29486 [anonymous French liturgical organ pieces, ca. 1618].

Nivers, Guillaume-Gabriel. *Dissertation sur le chant grégorien.* Paris: author, 1683.

*Livres d'orgue.* Vols. I and II, Paris: Robert Ballard, 1665; modern edition, ed. Norbert Dufourcq. Paris: Éditions Bornemann, 1963; vol. III, Paris: Robert Ballard, 1675; modern edition, ed. Norbert Dufourcq. Paris: Heugel, 1958.

*Traité de la composition de musique.* Paris: Robert Ballard, 1667; trans. and ed. Albert Cohen. Brooklyn, New York: Institute of Mediaeval Music, 1961.

Ozanam, Jacques. *Dictionnaire mathématique.* Paris: E. Michallet, 1691. [pp. 640–72: *Musique*]

Parran, Antoine. *Traité de la musique théorique et pratique.* Paris: Pierre Ballard, 1639; second edition, Paris: Robert Ballard, 1646; facsimile of the 1639 edition, Geneva: Minkoff Reprint, 1972.

Penna, Lorenzo. *Li primi albori musicali.* Bologna: P. M. Monti, 1672; facsimile of the 1696 edition, Bologna: Forni Editore, 1969.

Praetorius, Michael. *Syntagma Musicum.* vol. I, Wittenburg: Johannes

# Bibliography

Richter, 1615; vol. II, Wolfenbüttel: Elias Holwein, 1619; vol. III, Wolfenbüttel: Elias Holwein, 1619; facsimile editions, Afterwords by Wilibald Gurlitt. Kassel: Bärenreiter, 1958, 1958, 1959; trans. vol. I, Michael Fleming. Unpublished dissertation, Washington University, 1979; trans. vol. II (*De Organographia*), parts I and II, Harold Blumenfeld. New York: Da Capo Press, 1980; trans. vol. II, Parts I and II, David Crookes. Oxford: Oxford University Press, 1986; trans. vol. III, Hans Lampl. Unpublished dissertation, University of Southern California, 1957.

*Theatrum Instrumentorum.* Facsimile of the 1620 Wolfenbüttel edition, appended to vol. II of the *Syntagma Musicum*. Kassel: Bärenreiter, 1958.

Raison, André. *Livre d'orgue contenant cinq messes.* Paris: author, 1688; modern edition, ed. Alexandre Guilmant and André Pirro. Paris: A. Durand et Fils, 1899; modern edition, ed. Norbert Dufourcq. Paris: Éditions de la Schola Cantorum, 1963.

Rameau, Jean-Philippe. *Nouveau système de musique théorique.* Paris: Jean-Baptiste Ballard, 1726.

Ramos de Pareja, Bartolomeo. *Musica practica.* Bologna: Enrico di Colonia, Baltasar de Hiriberia, 1482; facsimile edition, Introduction by G. Vecchi. Bologna: Forni Editore, 1969.

Richelet, Pierre. *Dictionnaire françois.* Geneva: J. H. Widerhold, 1679–80; facsimile edition, Geneva: Slatkine Reprints, 1970.

Roberday, François [ed.?]. *Fugues, et caprices, à quatre parties mises en partition pour l'orgue.* Paris: Sanlecque, 1660; modern edition, ed. Jean Ferrard. Paris: Heugel, 1972.

Roberval, Gilles Personne de. 'Elementa musicae' (1651). MS Paris: Bibliothèque Nationale, fonds fr. 9119, fols. 374–470$^v$.

Rousseau, Jean. *Traité de la viole.* Paris: Christophe Ballard, 1687; facsimile edition, Geneva: Minkoff Reprint, 1975.

Roussier, Pierre-Joseph. *Mémoire sur le nouveau clavecin chromatique de M. de Laborde.* Paris: Philippe-Denys Pierres, 1782; facsimile in *Textes sur les instruments de musique au XVIII$^e$ siècle*. Geneva: Minkoff Reprint, 1972.

Saint Lambert, M. de. *Les principes du clavecin.* Paris: Christophe Ballard, 1702; facsimile edition, Geneva: Minkoff Reprint, 1974; trans. and ed. Rebecca Harris-Warrick. Cambridge: Cambridge University Press, 1984.

Salinas, Francisco de. *De musica libri septem.* Salamanca: Mathias Gastius, 1577; facsimile edition, ed. M. S. Kastner. Kassel: Bärenreiter, 1958.

Sancta María, Tomás de. *Libro llamado arte de tañer fantasia.* Valladolid: Francisco Fernandez de Cordova, 1565; facsimile edition, Geneva: Minkoff Reprint, 1973.

Sauveur, Joseph. 'Methode générale pour former les systêmes temperés de musique, & du choix de celui qu'on doit suivre', *Histoire de l'Académie royale des sciences* [1707], *Mémoires*, 203–22. Paris: Gabriel Martin et al., 1730.

# Bibliography

'Table générale des sistemes temperez de musique', *Histoire de l'Académie royale des sciences* [1711], *Mémoires*, 307–15. Paris: L'Imprimerie royale, 1730.
Facsimile reprints in *Joseph Sauveur: Collected Writings on Musical Acoustics*, ed. Rudolf Rasch. Utrecht: The Diapason Press, 1984.

Schlick, Arnolt. *Spiegel der Orgelmacher und Organisten*. Mainz: Peter Schöffer [the younger], 1511; facsimile edition, transcribed, trans. and ed. Elizabeth Barber. Buren, Netherlands: Frits Knuf, 1980.
*Tabulaturen etlicher Lobgesang und Lidlein uff die Orgeln und Lauten*. Mainz: Peter Schöffer [the younger], 1512; modern edition, *Arnolt Schlick, Orgelkompositionen*, ed. Rudolf Walter. Mainz: B. Schott's Söhne, 1970.

Sonnet, Martin. *Caeremoniale Parisiense ad usum omnium ecclesiarum, collegiatarum, parochialium & aliarum urbis & dioecesis Parisiensis*. Paris, 1662.

Titelouze, Jehan. *Hymnes de l'Eglise pour toucher sur l'orgue, avec les fugues et recherches sur leur plain-chant*. Paris: Pierre Ballard, 1623; modern edition, ed. Alexandre Guilmant and André Pirro. Paris: A. Durand et Fils, 1898; modern edition, ed. Norbert Dufourcq. Paris: Éditions Bornemann, 1965.
*Le Magnificat ou cantique de la Vierge pour toucher sur l'orgue, suivant les huit tons de l'Eglise*. Paris: Pierre Ballard, 1626; modern edition, ed. Alexandre Guilmant and André Pirro. Paris: A. Durand et Fils, 1898.
Facsimile edition of both volumes, Geneva: Minkoff Reprint, 1985.

Trichet, Pierre. *Traité des instruments de musique* [ca. 1640]. MS Paris: Bibliothèque Sainte-Geneviève, ms. 1070; modern edition, ed. François Lesure. Neuilly-sur-Seine: Société de musique d'autrefois, 1957; reprinted Geneva: Minkoff Reprint, 1978.

Vicentino, Nicola. *L'antica musica ridotta alla moderna prattica*. Rome: Antonio Barre, 1555; facsimile edition, ed. Edward Lowinsky. Kassel: Bärenreiter, 1959.

Werckmeister, Andreas. *Erweiterte und verbesserte Orgel-Probe*. Quedlinburg: Theodor Calvisius and Johann Sievert, 1698; facsimile edition, ed. Dietz-Rüdiger Moser. Kassel: Bärenreiter, 1970; trans. Gerhard Krapf. Raleigh: The Sunbury Press, 1976.
*Musicalische Temperatur*. Quedlinburg: Theodor Calvisius, 1691; facsimile edition, ed. Rudolf Rasch. Utrecht: Diapason Press, 1983.

Yssandon, Jean. *Traité de la musique pratique*. Paris: Adrian Le Roy and Robert Ballard, 1582; facsimile edition, Geneva: Minkoff Reprint, 1972.

Zarlino, Gioseffo. *Dimostrationi harmoniche*. Venice: Francesco de 'Franceschi, Senese, 1571; facsimile of the 1573 edition, Ridgewood, New Jersey: Gregg Press, 1966.
*Le istitutioni harmoniche*. Venice: Francesco de 'Franceschi, Senese, 1558; facsimile of the 1573 edition, New York: Broude Brothers, 1965; facsimile of the 1573 edition, Ridgewood, New Jersey: Gregg Press, 1966.

# Bibliography

## NINETEENTH- AND TWENTIETH-CENTURY SOURCES

Aldrich, Putnam. 'The principal agréments of the seventeenth and eighteenth centuries; a study in musical ornamentation'. Unpublished dissertation, Harvard University, 1942.

Anthony, James. *French Baroque Music from Beaujoyeulx to Rameau.* Revised edition, New York: W. W. Norton, 1978.

Apel, Willi. *Geschichte der Orgel- und Klaviermusik bis 1700.* Kassel: Bärenreiter, 1967; trans. and revised Hans Tischler as *The History of Keyboard Music to 1700.* Bloomington: Indiana University Press, 1972.

'Probleme der Alternierung in der liturgischen Orgelmusik bis 1600', in *Claudio Monteverdi e il suo tempo,* ed. Raffaello Monterosso. Verona: Stamperia Valdonega, 1969.

Asselin, Pierre-Yves. 'Le tempérament en France au 18$^e$ siècle', in *L'Orgue à notre époque,* ed. Donald Mackey. Montreal: McGill University, 1981.

Atcherson, Walter. 'Key and Mode in Seventeenth-Century Music Theory Books', *Journal of Music Theory* xvii (1973), 204–32.

Barbour, Murray. 'Irregular Systems of Temperament', *Journal of the American Musicological Society* i (1948), 20–6.

*Tuning and Temperament, a Historical Survey.* Second edition, East Lansing: Michigan State College Press, 1953.

Barnes, John. 'The Specious Uniformity of Italian Harpsichords', in *Keyboard Instruments: Studies in Keyboard Organology,* ed. Edwin Ripin. Edinburgh: Edinburgh University Press, 1971; reprint edition, New York: Dover Publications, 1977.

Bénoit, Marcelle. *Versailles et les musiciens du roi, 1661–1733.* Paris: Éditions A. et J. Picard, 1971.

Berger, Karol. *Theories of Chromatic and Enharmonic Music in Late 16th Century Italy.* Ann Arbor: UMI Research Press, 1980.

Blackwood, Easley. *The Structure of Recognizable Diatonic Tunings.* Princeton: Princeton University Press, 1985.

Boalch, Donald H. *Makers of the Harpsichord and Clavichord 1440–1840.* Second edition, Oxford: The Clarendon Press, 1974.

Bonfils, Jean. 'L'Oeuvre d'orgue de Jehan Titelouze', *Recherches sur la musique française classique* v (1965), 5–16.

Bouvet, Charles. 'Quelques précisions biographiques sur Louis et Charles Couperin', *Revue de Musicologie* xxxiv (1930), 81–92.

Brenet, Michel [pseud. Marie Bobillier]. *Les Musiciens de la Sainte-Chapelle du Palais.* Paris: Librairie Alphonse Picard et Fils, 1910; reprint edition, Geneva: Minkoff Reprint, 1973.

Brossard, Yolande de, ed. *Musiciens de Paris 1535–1792: actes d'état civil.* Paris: Éditions A. et J. Picard, 1965.

Brown, Howard. *Embellishing Sixteenth-Century Music.* Oxford: Oxford University Press, 1976.

Brunold, Paul. *Traité des signes et agréments employés par les clavecinistes français.* Nice: Georges Delrieu, 1965.

115

# Bibliography

Bunjes, Paul. *The Praetorius Organ*. St Louis: Concordia Publishing House, 1966.

Caldwell, John. 'Sources of keyboard music to 1660: France', *The New Grove Dictionary of Music and Musicians* (1980), vol. xvii, 723–4.

Choquet, Gustave. 'Études sur les facteurs d'instruments-virtuoses: Richard, les frères Denis, M. Dumont', *Revue et gazette musicale de Paris* xxxxvii (16 May 1880), 154–6.

Cohen, Albert. 'A Study of Instrumental Ensemble Practice in Seventeenth-Century France', *Galpin Society Journal* xv (1962), 3–17.

'Marin Mersenne', *The New Grove Dictionary of Music and Musicians* (1980), vol. xii, 188–90.

'Survivals of Renaissance Thought in French Theory 1610–1670: A Bibliographical Study', in *Aspects of Medieval and Renaissance Music (A Birthday Offering to Gustave Reese)*, 82–95. New York: W. W. Norton, 1966; reprint edition, New York: Pendragon Press, 1978.

'Symposium on Seventeenth-Century Music Theory: France' (with a Checklist of Sources), *Journal of Music Theory* xvi (1972), 16–35.

Connolly, Thomas. 'Psalm' (II), *The New Grove Dictionary of Music and Musicians* (1980), vol. xv, 322–32.

Curtis, Alan. 'Musique classique française à Berkeley, pièces inédites de Louis Couperin, Lebègue, La Barre, etc.', *Revue de Musicologie* lvi (1970), 123–64.

Dalhaus, Carl. 'Zu Costeleys chromatischer Chanson', *Die Musikforschung* xvi (1963), 253–65.

Daniels, Arthur. 'Microtonality and Mean-Tone Temperament in the Harmonic System of Francisco Salinas', *Journal of Music Theory* ix (1965), 2–51 and 234–80.

De Boer, Barbara. 'The Harpsichord Music of Jean-Nicolas Geoffroy'. Unpublished dissertation, Northwestern University, 1983.

Dombois, Eugen. 'Varieties of Meantone Temperament Realized on the Lute', *Journal of the Lute Society of America* vii (1974), 82–9.

Douglass, Fenner. *The Language of the Classical French Organ*. New Haven: Yale University Press, 1969.

Dufourcq, Norbert. 'De l'emploi du temps de organistes Parisiens sous les règnes de Louis XIII et Louis XIV', *La Revue Musicale* ccxxvi (1955), 35–47.

*La musique d'orgue française de Jehan Titelouze à Jehan Alain*. Second edition, Paris: Librairie Floury, 1949.

*Le livre de l'orgue français*. 5 vols: Tome I, *Les sources (Documents inédits)*; Tome II, *Le buffet*; Tome III, *La facture*; Tome IV, *La musique*; Tome V, *Miscellanea*. Paris: Éditions A. et J. Picard, 1968–82.

*Nicolas Lebègue*. Paris: Éditions A. et J. Picard, 1954.

'Recent Researches into French Organ-Building from the Fifteenth to the Seventeenth Century', *Galpin Society Journal* x (1957), 66–81.

Dupont, Wilhelm. *Geschichte der musikalischen Temperatur*. Nördlingen: C. H. Beck'sche Buchdruckerei, 1935.

# Bibliography

Écorcheville, Jules Armand Joseph. *Actes d'état civil de musiciens insinuées au Châtelet de Paris (1539–1650)*. Paris: L. M. Fortin, 1907. [Information only on Denis family members other than Jean II]

Elders, Willem. 'Zur Formtechnik in Titelouzes *Hymnes de l'Église*', *Die Musikforschung* xviii (1965), 403–12.

Evans, Jeffrey. 'The keyboard tuning rules of *The Modern Musick-master*', *Early Music* xi (1983), 360–3.

Frotscher, Gotthold. *Geschichte des Orgelspiels und der Orgelkomposition*. Berlin: Max Hesses Verlag, 1935.

Fuller, David. 'An unknown French ornament table from 1699', *Early Music* ix (1981), 55–61.

'Eighteenth-Century French Harpsichord Music'. Unpublished dissertation, Harvard University, 1965. [Chapter One: 'Seventeenth-Century French Harpsichord Music']

'French harpsichord playing in the 17th century – *after Le Gallois*', *Early Music* iv (1976), 22–6.

Gastoué, Amédée. *L'Orgue en France, de l'antiquité au début de la période classique*. Paris: Éditions de la Schola Cantorum, 1921.

'Note sur la généalogie et la famille de l'organiste Titelouze (1563–1633)', *Revue de Musicologie* xxxv (1930), 171–5.

Godt, Irving. 'Guillaume Costeley: Life and Works'. Unpublished dissertation, New York University, 1969.

Gruber, Albion. 'Evolving Tonal Theory in Seventeenth-Century France'. Unpublished dissertation, Eastman School of Music, University of Rochester, 1969.

'Mersenne and Evolving Tonal Theory', *Journal of Music Theory* xiv (1970), 36–67.

Gustafson, Bruce. *French Harpsichord Music of the 17th Century: a Thematic Catalog of the Sources with Commentary*. 3 vols. Ann Arbor: UMI Research Press, 1979.

Hammond, Frederick. *Girolamo Frescobaldi*. Cambridge, Mass.: Harvard University Press, 1983.

Hardouin, Pierre. 'Denis', in *Larousse de la musique*, vol. I, 260. Paris: Librairie Larousse, 1957.

'François Roberday (1624–1680)', *Revue de Musicologie* xlv (1960), 44–62.

'La composition des orgues que pouvaient toucher les musiciens parisiens aux alentours de 1600', in *La musique instrumentale de la Renaissance*. Paris: Éditions du Centre National de la Recherche Scientifique, 1955.

'Notes biographiques sur quelques organistes parisiens des XVII^e et XVIII^e siècles: Florent Bienvenu', *L'Orgue* lxxxii (January–March 1957), 1–7.

Higginbottom, Edward. 'Ecclesiastical Prescription and Musical Style in French Classical Organ Music', *The Organ Yearbook* xii (1981), 31–54.

'French Classical Organ Music and the Liturgy', *Proceedings of the Royal Musical Association* ciii (1976–7), 19–40.

# Bibliography

'The Liturgy and French Classical Organ Music'. Unpublished dissertation, Cambridge University, 1979.

Hirt, Franz Josef. *Meisterwerke des Klavierbaues*. Olten, Switzerland: Urs Graf-Verlag, 1955; trans. M. Boehme-Brown as *Stringed Keyboard Instruments 1440–1880*. Boston: Boston Book and Art Shop, 1968.

Hoag, Barbara. 'A Spanish Clavichord Tuning of the Seventeenth Century', *Journal of the American Musical Instrument Society* ii (1976), 86–95.

Horsley, Imogene. *Fugue, History and Practice*. New York: The Free Press, 1966.

'Symposium on Seventeenth-Century Music Theory: Italy', *Journal of Music Theory* xvi (1972), 50–9.

Howell, Almonte. 'French Baroque Organ Music and the Eight Church Tones', *Journal of the American Musicological Society* xi (1959), 106–18.

'The French Organ Mass in the Sixteenth and Seventeenth Centuries'. Unpublished dissertation, University of North Carolina, 1953.

'Titelouze', *The New Grove Dictionary of Music and Musicians* (1980), vol. xix, 13–14.

Howell, Standley. 'Ramos de Pareja's "Brief Discussion of Various Instruments"', *Journal of the American Musical Instrument Society* xi (1985), 14–37.

Hubbard, Frank. 'The *Encyclopédie* and the French Harpsichord', *Galpin Society Journal* ix (1956), 37–50.

*Three Centuries of Harpsichord Making*. Cambridge, Mass.: Harvard University Press, 1965.

Hughes, Andrew. 'Solmization' (I), *The New Grove Dictionary of Music and Musicians* (1980), vol. xvii, 458–9.

Huguet, Edmond, ed. *Dictionnaire de la langue française du seizième siècle*. 7 vols. Paris: Eduard Champion, 1925–73.

Husmann, Heinrich. 'Zur Charakteristik der Schlickschen Temperatur', *Archiv für Musikwissenschaft* xxiv (1967), 253–65.

Hyde, Frederick. 'The Position of Marin Mersenne in the History of Music'. Unpublished dissertation, Yale University, 1954.

Jorgensen, Owen. *Tuning the Historical Temperaments by Ear*. Marquette, Michigan: Northern Michigan University Press, 1977.

Jurgens, Madeleine, ed. *Documents du Minutier central concernant l'histoire de la musique* (1600–50). 2 vols., Preface by François Lesure. Paris: La Documentation Française, 1969, 1974.

Kaufmann, Henry. 'More on the Tuning of the *Archicembalo*', *Journal of the American Musicological Society* xxiii (1970), 84–94.

*The life and works of Nicola Vicentino, 1511–c. 1576*. Rome: American Institute of Musicology, 1966.

'Vicentino's Arciorgano: an Annotated Translation', *Journal of Music Theory* v (1961), 32–53.

Kitchen, John. 'Harpsichord Music of Seventeenth-Century France: The Forms, Their Origins and Development, with Particular Emphasis on the

# Bibliography

Work of Louis Couperin'. Unpublished dissertation, Cambridge University, 1979.

Klotz, Hans. *Über die Orgelkunst der Gotik, der Renaissance und des Barock.* Kassel: Bärenreiter, 1975.

La Chesnaye-Desbois, François Aubert de. *Dictionnaire de la noblesse.* 19 vols. Paris: Schlesinger Frères, 1863–77; facsimile edition in 10 vols., Nancy: Berger-Levrault, 1980.

Lange, Helmut. 'Über die Bedeutung des syntonischen Kommas und seine Verwendung in der Orgelstimmung Gottfried Silbermanns', *Acta Organologica* xvi (1982), 235–48.

Larousse, Pierre. *Grand dictionnaire universel.* 18 vols. Paris: Administration du Grand Dictionnaire Universel, 1874.

Launay, Denise. 'Essai d'un commentaire de Titelouze par lui-même', *Recherches sur la musique française classique* v (1965), 27–50.

Le Huray, Peter. 'Fingering' (I, 1–3), *The New Grove Dictionary of Music and Musicians* (1980), vol. vi, 567–72.

Le Moel, Michel. 'Les dernières années de J. Champion de Chambonnières', *Recherches sur la musique française classique* i (1960), 31–46.

Lesure, François. 'Denis, Familie', *MGG*, vol. iii, 160–3.

'Denis', *The New Grove Dictionary of Music and Musicians* (1980), vol. v, 363–4.

'La facture instrumentale à Paris au seizième siècle', *Galpin Society Journal* vii (1954), 11–52; reprinted in *Musique et musiciens français du XVIᵉ siècle* (collected articles 1950–69). Geneva: Minkoff Reprint, 1976.

Levy, Kenneth. 'Costeley's Chromatic Chanson', in *Annales musicologiques, Moyen-Age et Renaissance*, vol. iii, 213–63. Neuilly-sur-Seine: Société de musique d'autrefois, 1955.

Lindley, Mark. 'Early 16th-Century Keyboard Temperaments', *Musica Disciplina* xxviii (1974), 129–51.

'Fifteenth-Century Evidence for Meantone Temperament', *Proceedings of the Royal Musical Association* cii (1975–6), 37–51.

'Instructions for the Clavier Diversely Tempered', *Early Music* v (1977), 18–23.

*Lutes, Viols and Temperaments.* Cambridge: Cambridge University Press, 1984.

'Mean-tone', *The New Grove Dictionary of Music and Musicians* (1980), vol. xi, 875.

'Mersenne on Keyboard Tuning', *Journal of Music Theory* xxiv (1980), 167–203.

'Stimmung und Temperatur', in *Geschichte der Musiktheorie* VI, ed. F. Zaminer. Darmstadt: Wissenschaftliche Buchgesellschaft, forthcoming.

'Temperaments' and related articles, *The New Grove Dictionary of Music and Musicians* (1980), vol. xviii, 660–74.

Lister, Craig. 'Traditions of Keyboard Technique from 1650 to 1750'. Unpublished dissertation, University of North Carolina, 1979.

# Bibliography

Lloyd, Llewellyn and Hugh Boyle. *Intervals, Scales and Temperaments.* Second edition, New York: St Martin's Press, 1979.

Loubet de Sceaury, Paul. *Musiciens et facteurs d'instruments de musique sous l'ancien régime.* Paris: Éditions A. Pedone, 1949.

Mandelbaum, Joel. 'Multiple Division of the Octave and the Tonal Resources of 19-Tone Temperament'. Unpublished dissertation, Indiana University, 1961.

Marcuse, Sybil. *A Survey of Musical Instruments.* New York: Harper and Row, 1975.

Martin, Lynn. 'The Colonna-Stella *Sambuca lincea*, An Enharmonic Keyboard Instrument', *Journal of the American Musical Instrument Society* x (1984), 5–21.

Massip, Catherine. *La vie des musiciens de Paris au temps de Mazarin.* Paris: Éditions A. et J. Picard, 1976.

McGeary, Thomas. 'Early Eighteenth-Century English Harpsichord Tuning and Stringing', *English Harpsichord Magazine* iii (1982), 18–22.

Meeùs, Nicolas. 'Renaissance Transposing Keyboard Instruments', *Fellowship of Makers and Researchers of Historical Instruments Quarterly* vi and vii (1977), 18–26, 16–24.

Mendel, Arthur. 'Devices for Transposition in the Organ before 1600', *Acta Musicologica* xxi (1949), 24–40.

Moroney, Davitt. 'The performance of unmeasured harpsichord preludes', *Early Music* iv (1976), 143–51.

Nerici, Luigi. *Storia della musica in Lucca.* Lucca: Tipographia Giusti, 1879.

Neumann, Frederick. *Ornamentation in Baroque and Post-Baroque Music, with Special Emphasis on J. S. Bach.* Princeton: Princeton University Press, 1978.

Oldham, Guy. 'Louis Couperin: A New Source of French Keyboard Music of the Mid 17th Century', *Recherches sur la musique française classique* i (1960), 51–9.

Palisca, Claude. 'The Beginnings of Baroque Music; Its Roots in Sixteenth Century Theory and Polemics'. Unpublished dissertation, Harvard University, 1953.

Parker, Mildred. 'Some Speculations on the French Keyboard Suites of the Seventeenth and Early Eighteenth Centuries', *International Review of the Aesthetics and Sociology of Music* vii (1976), 203–17.

Parkins, Robert. 'Keyboard fingering in early Spanish sources', *Early Music* xi (1983), 323–31.

Pierre, Constant. *Les facteurs d'instruments de musique.* Facsimile of the 1893 Paris edition. Geneva: Minkoff Reprint, 1971.

Pirro, André. *Les organistes français du XVII<sup>e</sup> siècle: Jehan Titelouze.* (Conférence prononcée dans la salle de la Société Saint-Jean, le 24 mars 1898). Paris: Au Bureaux de la Schola Cantorum, n.d.

Powell, Newman. 'Rhythmic Freedom in the Performance of French Music from 1650 to 1735'. Unpublished dissertation, Stanford University, 1958.

# Bibliography

Powers, Harold. 'Mode', *The New Grove Dictionary of Music and Musicians* (1980), vol. xii, 376–418.

Pruitt, William. 'Bibliographie des oeuvres de Nivers', *Recherches sur la musique française classique* xiii (1973), 133–56.

'The Organ Works of Guillaume-Gabriel Nivers', *Recherches sur la musique française classique* xiv (1974), 5–81 and xv (1975), 47–79.

'The Organ Works of Guillaume-Gabriel Nivers'. Unpublished dissertation, University of Pittsburgh, 1969.

'Un traité d'interpretation du XVII$^e$ siècle', *L'Orgue* clii (1974), 99–111.

Quittard, Henri. 'Un claveciniste du XVII$^e$ siècle, Jacques Champion de Chambonnières', *La Tribune de Saint Gervais* vii (1901), 1–11, 33–44, 71–7, 105–10, 141–9.

Raugel, Félix. *Les grandes orgues des églises de Paris*. Paris: Librairie Fischbacher, 1927.

Reimann, Margarete. *Untersuchungen zur Formgeschichte der französischen Klavier-Suite*. Regensburg: Gustav Bosse Verlag, 1940.

Ripin, Edwin. 'The French Harpsichord Before 1650', *Galpin Society Journal* xx (1967), 43–7.

'The Two-Manual Harpsichord in Flanders Before 1650', *Galpin Society Journal* xxi (1968), 33–9.

Roche, Martine. 'Un livre de clavecin français de la fin du XVII$^e$ siècle', *Recherches sur la musique française classique* vii (1967), 39–73.

Rokseth, Yvonne. *La musique d'orgue au XV$^e$ siècle et au debut du XVI$^e$*. Paris: Librairie E. Droz, 1930.

Russell, Raymond. *The Harpsichord and Clavichord*. London: Faber and Faber, 1959; rev. Howard Schott. London: Faber and Faber, 1973.

Samoyault-Verlet, Colombe. *Les facteurs de clavecins parisiens, notices biographiques et documents (1550–1793)*. Paris: Société Française de Musicologie (Heugel), 1966.

Scheibert, Beverly. *Jean-Henry D'Anglebert and the Seventeenth-Century Clavecin School*. Bloomington: Indiana University Press, 1986.

Schneider, Herbert. *Die französische Kompositionslehre in der ersten Hälfte des 17. Jahrhunderts*. Tutzing: Hans Schneider, 1972.

Servières, G. *Documents inédits sur les organistes françaises des XVII$^e$ et XVIII$^e$ siècles*. Paris: Éditions de la Schola Cantorum, 1922.

Shannon, John. *Organ Literature of the Seventeenth Century*. Raleigh: The Sunbury Press, 1978.

Smith, Anne. 'Über Modus und Transposition um 1600', in *Basler Jahrbuch für historische Musikpraxis* VI (1982). Winterthur, Switzerland: Amadeus Verlag, 1983.

Steblin, Rita. *A History of Key Characteristics in the Eighteenth and Early Nineteenth Centuries*. Ann Arbor: UMI Research Press, 1983.

Tolkoff, Lynn. 'French Modal Theory before Rameau', *Journal of Music Theory* xvii (1973), 150–63.

Vanmackelberg, Dom M. 'Autour de Jehan Titelouze', *Recherches sur la musique française classique* iv (1964), 5–32.

# Bibliography

Van Wye, Benjamin. 'Ritual Use of the Organ in France', *Journal of the American Musicological Society* xxxiii (1980), 287–325.

Verchaly, André. 'La musique religieuse française de Titelouze à 1660', *La Revue Musicale* ccxxii (1953–4), 77–88.

Vogan, Charles. 'French Organ School of the Seventeenth and Eighteenth Centuries'. Unpublished dissertation, University of Michigan, 1949.

Vogel, Harald. 'Tuning and Temperament in the North German School of the Seventeenth and Eighteenth Centuries', in *Charles Brenton Fisk, Organbuilder* vol. I. Easthampton, Mass.: The Westfield Center for Early Keyboard Studies, 1986.

Williams, Peter. 'Equal Temperament and the English Organ, 1675–1825', *Acta Musicologica* xl (1968), 53–65.

*The European Organ*. London: Batsford, 1966.

*A New History of the Organ*. Bloomington: Indiana University Press, 1980.

Wright, Rowland. *Dictionnaire des instruments de musique*. London: Battley Brothers, 1941.

# Index

123

# Index

# Index

# Index

# Index

# Index

triads, major, in quarter-comma meantone, 31
Trichet, Pierre, 24n, 52
trill, 98, 99, 100
tritone, 62n
tuning
    just, 15, 17, 36, 62n
    of harpsichords, 12, 25–6, 27, 29–30, 31, 64, 65–9, 71–2
    of organs, 12, 24–6, 29–30, 43, 64, 71–2
    Pythagorean, 15, 64n, 66n

*Ut queant laxis* hymn, 96

Van Wye, Benjamin, 44n
Varzy, Musée de, 7
verset, 44–50, 89
Vespers, 45

Vicentino, Nicola, 36, 67n, 68n
viols, 39, 64n, 68–9
virginal, 51
Vivonne, Duc de, 13

Weimar, 39
Werckmeister, Andreas, 17n, 22, 40
whole tones, in meantone temperaments, 16–17, 24n, 60, 67–8
Williams, Peter, 40n, 70n
Wolfenbüttel, 39
'wolf' fifth, 17, 18, 66n
wrist, position of in keyboard playing, 97

Yssandon, Jean, 52n

Zarlino, Gioseffo, 19, 20, 22